CHUCK AND ANGELA FAZIO

OWNERS/BROKER, OVER $5 BILLION IN PRODUCTION

MASTERING

— YOUR —

REAL ESTATE
CAREER

YOUR BLUEPRINT TO MOVE
FROM STRUGGLE TO SUCCESS

MASTERING YOUR REAL ESTATE CAREER

Your Blueprint to Move from Struggle to Success

ENDORSEMENTS

Chuck and Angela Fazio are leaders and trend-setters in the real estate industry. Realtors everywhere will benefit from them sharing a bit of their expertise through this book. They really care about the industry and are committed to the growth of agents everywhere. Relationship is what drives real estate and these two have got it nailed!

-Jay Kinder

Jay and I like to partner with quality people. We consider Chuck and Angela Fazio our partners. I believe you should give everything you have out of everything that you've got. In this book you will see that Chuck and Angela do just that!

-Michael Reese

Jay Kinder and Michael Reese have sold thousands of homes in their career and are nationally acclaimed trainers and mentors. They are published authors and founders of the National Association of Expert Advisors (NAEA)

TABLE OF CONTENTS

FOREWORD

I never dreamed that I'd end up in this place in my life—so extremely and intensely blessed. Writing this book with my sweet husband has brought our blessings into laser focus. It was also great fun. My husband will tell you, and I'll agree, that I'm a nerd and sometimes a little corny. Although we worked together on the whole book, I composed most of it in the way I write. So when you come across the nerdy, corny parts . . . don't blame Chuck.

We hope to bring you, the reader, through our story so that at the end, you will have laughed and pondered, considered, and ultimately experienced some truth. Real estate is a passion for us and the Lord has surely blessed us to be exceedingly excellent in our career.

It's important for you to know where we came from to understand where we are now. I met Chuck my first year in real estate. The first six months of Chuck and I working real estate together was super hard, and we nearly failed. In fact, we were failures. Now, with our vast experience, we know that most agents would have given up. We didn't. That next year (our first full year working together), we sold over $11 million in real estate. In our second, third and fourth years we sold $17.5, $22 and almost $40 million—just the two of us. In that fourth year, our team sold almost $89 million.

In our fifth year, we opened our own brokerage. According to the Phoenix Business Journal, our brokerage was ranked in the top brokerages in 2006, our first full year of business, along with every year since then for the entire twelve years we've been open.

For the last several years, we have owned and operated a real estate school where people can get licensed to be agents and where agents can get training. Our school has impressive pass rate statistics for pre-licensing and some of the best instructors in the industry.

Because we've transacted and overseen so much business, coached and mentored hundreds of agents, and owned a successful real estate school—watching brand-new agents out of the gate—we have come up with one of the best blueprints of what makes an agent successful or unsuccessful.

If it is a successful career in real estate you're looking for, we will show you some of the most important qualities you will need in order to make it. If you are looking for success in life in general, we can help with that too. It's never too late to change your circumstances. Here is our story.

INTRODUCTION

Mastering Your Real Estate Career was written for several groups of people:

Those who are considering a career in real estate: This blueprint will help you to gain insight into what you will be up against when entering into this career. It will cause you to consider if you are willing to do what will be necessary for success.

Those who are brand new to real estate: If you're brand new, we will help you to get started with the right expectations and save you time and energy trying to reinvent the wheel. We'll step you through the foundational principles of success when it comes to real estate. You'll learn from two people who know what it takes to push through the challenges and come out on the other side with success.

Those who are struggling in real estate: Struggles in real estate are inevitable. It is a taxing industry, but offers great reward. For the struggling real estate agent, we will help you to be aware of roadblocks that you may be experiencing and give you sound strategies to overcome them. We offer practical knowledge and encouragement to persevere.

Those who are looking to get to the next level in their real estate career: Real estate is a fantastic career with great potential for success, financially, relationally and in satisfaction of achievement. When you want to get to the next level in your career, sometimes all it takes is a quarter turn in one or more areas to open up your possibilities. We'll offer insight into sharpening your skills and working on your mindset that will cause you to catapult your career in a way that you haven't experienced before.

———

No matter which group describes you, I encourage you to read every chapter. The most successful people constantly review the basics. Even the most experienced agents may have forgotten to apply some of the foundational principles to their businesses or perhaps you stumbled through the beginning part of your career, like we did, and never had the expert guidance to build your business in the highest and best way. For the struggling or experienced agent, read with brand-new eyes and an open mind. As was stated above, small changes can make big differences in your success. For all of you, keep reading and enjoy the ride!

CHAPTER ONE

OUR INTERESTING JOURNEYS THAT LED US INTO REAL ESTATE

"I was a bilingual teacher with a double masters and a side job as a Denver Broncos cheerleader..."

—ANGELA FAZIO

People have asked me, "How did you get into real estate?" I wish I had a super interesting answer like, "Houses have always been my passion, and sales is in my blood." Or maybe, "My parents were REALTORS® and my parents' parents were REALTORS®" . . . but the truth is, I don't really know for sure.

I was a school teacher for about seven years, teaching nearly every elementary grade from Kindergarten to sixth grade. I absolutely loved my work and poured my heart and soul into it. In fact, that's really my personality. I'm a bit of an extremist. When I approach a task or an idea, I tend to go overboard. Mediocre has never been my MO.

Another quality of mine is that I *love* to work. Even during my teaching years I had other jobs. Waitressing made the list as well as twisting balloons, private tutoring and cheerleading for the Denver Broncos.

No, I'm not a huge fan of football. It wasn't my life-long dream to be an NFL cheerleader. The true story is that I was involved in a car crash which gave me a headache that lasted a year and a half. During this time, I saw chiropractors, physical therapists, relaxation therapists and a massage therapist named Marie. Besides being one of the most beautiful women I'd ever met, she was also a Denver Nuggets dancer.

She learned, over time, that I used to dance as a child and somehow, she decided that was a good enough background to try out with her for the Denver Broncos Cheerleaders. Never mind that I hadn't danced in ten years. I thought to myself, "*why not?*" Apparently, I had no fear and a confidence level I probably shouldn't have possessed.

I showed up not too long afterwards at the first day of tryouts. We had to bring a headshot. I'm pretty sure I was one of the only girls without a professional headshot and, even though I was only twenty-six, I was one of the oldest girls there, too.

Tryouts were grueling, and it was only the first of the two days of tryouts. At the end of the first day, the most dramatic cuts were made. I didn't make the cut. I went home exhausted and sad. That was Sunday.

On Monday morning, I was back at school teaching my fourth-grade class. All morning, it bothered me that I didn't make the cut. In fact, I started to get a bit aggravated, thinking, *"They don't know what they're missing!"*

Not one to give up, I actually left the school during my lunch break and drove down to the Broncos facility. I asked for the director of the cheerleaders, who happened to be in her office. She let me talk with her, and I told her very humbly that I believed there had been a mistake. I should not have been cut. I would be an amazing asset to the team. I explained that as a school teacher, I was well-spoken and having me represent the Broncos cheerleaders would be an advantage. I asked for a second chance.

The director looked at me for a few seconds. Then she wrote down a phone number and told me to call and get in on a private practice session. I did not give up.

Truth be told, I was not the best dancer on the team, and I had to practice five times as hard as anyone else. It was the first time in my life I had to work that hard to *not* be the best. It was humbling and a great life lesson. At the end of the season, not only did I earn a Super Bowl ring but also the title of "Rookie of the Year." They sent me to Austria with a group of NFL cheerleaders from across the nation as an ambassador for the Broncos; it was the first time a rookie was ever chosen to go on such a trip. That football season was not only a whole lot of fun, but I got to wear chaps!

That same year, I moved back to Arizona and had my first child. I decided I would be a stay-at-home mom and even joined "Mommy's Groups." If you actually knew me, you would be laughing right out loud. Being a stay-at-home mom was terrible for me. I have no idea how women can do that. They are true saints! God created me to work *outside* the home. I went a little crazy for sure! One year later, I found myself divorcing. Because I didn't want to be a broke single mother as a school teacher, I decided to give real estate a shot. That was March, 2001.

"I was a mailman, and I worked as a bouncer . . . "
—CHUCK FAZIO

This chapter is radical and not for the judgmental. I want to preface what you will read with the fact that I was brought up in New York by a good Italian family with parents who are still together today and that God did eventually get a hold of me and turn my life right-side up.

But things weren't always so good. Growing up, I hated school! I put more time and energy into how to beat the system than I did at learning. I mastered it. I went to one of the best boys' high schools in New York and still beat the system. Just to give you an idea of how good I was at it, I had five out of six F's the first semester of my senior year. In case you are curious, the sixth subject was gym, and I had an A. I graduated by being a master cheater and having a very good memory. I can study the night before a final and remember the material. What a gift from God. I can't explain how my brain works. I also mastered cutting out of school and going to Jones Beach, getting high and drinking while working on my tan.

At the age of eighteen, a friend of mine asked if I wanted a job bouncing at a club on Long Island. I thought, "Sure! A job where I can drink, hang out, get into fights and get paid? What a concept." Weekend after weekend, I watched the money flow into the club because it was packed all the time. I got an adrenaline rush due to at least six to seven brawls a night.

I quickly loved the idea of being a bouncer. I even took many years of Jiu Jitsu. I got offered a job being a bouncer at a new strip club in Manhattan, one of the first real strip clubs ever. Before that they were usually local dives. This was also my first exposure to the mob. What a life these people lived: beautiful women and lots of cash. Any given night, we would have these celebrities in the club. I was introduced to three things: drugs, the mafia and Hell's Angels.

During the same time, I got married to my first wife. We were young with different goals. Needless to say, I was a piece of crap for a husband. She deserved way better than me. The blessings were that I had two beautiful kids, Danielle and Charles. They had the best mother anyone could ask for but garbage, at that time, for a dad.

My life started to go into a downward spiral. I took a job as a mailman for the benefits, but my nights were filled with life in the clubs. The motto I started to adopt was, "I'd rather be feared than loved." Yes, I was officially a dirt bag. I quickly acclimated myself with this new crowd. I was a drug dealer and thrived on beating the crap out of jerks in the club. I was living in a very dark and demonic world.

I should have been dead ten times over. There were so many times that I would fall asleep at the wheel and wake up going 80 mph and heading straight for the divider. I had been threatened in the club hundreds of times by people telling me they would come back and kill me. I watched two of my friends get killed. I've had a hit put out on me, a knife to my throat, a gun to my head, and I've been jumped by a five-guy set-up.

Regardless, I kept working at the clubs. Any club I went into, people knew who I was. My crew and I were hired out to clean up problem clubs. I was self-centered and strived for fame at all costs. I modeled and appeared on shows like Ricki Lake, as Mr. April for the Male Hunk Calendar Contest, the Mark Wahlberg show, and Richard Bey. I was carted around in limos like a VIP.

I was always looking over my shoulder. A crappy husband and even worse father, I completely alienated my family. How much lower of a person could I have been?

But God had a plan.

In the end of 1998, I told my wife at the time that I wanted to move to Arizona.

All of my immediate family had moved already, and I was ready for a new start. This move was a huge thing to ask of my first wife as she would be leaving her entire family for the sake of the kids and the hope of a reconciliation that wouldn't happen.

I had no job and didn't want to get back into the club business.

What would I do? Real estate—yeah, that was the answer. I would be my own boss and make as much money as I wanted. So I got into real estate at the end of 1998 and had my license by January, 1999.

My first marriage ended about that time too, so I threw myself into my new career.

"The first words I ever said to my husband . . . "
—ANGELA

I absolutely love "how we met" stories. They fascinate me. I am especially jealous of the couples who have known each other forever and have been married a million years.

My husband is my best friend in every sense of the word. He's my soul mate. He's my business partner, and I still can't wait to go out on dates with him. Almost all of our time is spent together, and our marriage gets sweeter and sweeter every day. We've been married almost fifteen years, and I'm excited for the rest of my life with him. The Lord has ridiculously blessed us.

Chuck and I met in early March, 2001. It was my very first day in real estate, and I was ready to conquer the world. I walked into our team meeting that first day and took a seat near the front of the room. As the team meeting commenced, I was focused and attentive, concentrating on every word that was said.

Our team leaders were a husband and wife team. The wife was writing the team members' sales and listings on a large white board. Soon, I heard a booming voice with a thick New York accent shouting out, "Hey Nikki, you on a diet?"

I turned around to see where that voice was coming from. At the back of the room, in a sleeveless shirt and shorts, sat the man from whom the question originated. Nikki had, by then, given this man her full attention and replied with a wide smile, "Yes, can you tell?"

The booming voice responded, "Yeah. I can see the board now."

As a divorcing woman coming out of a not-so-fun situation, I immediately grew hot with anger. Without a single thought to what I was about to say, I turned to Mr. Booming Voice and shouted, "What are you, an a$$h@!e?" What followed was no less than a tongue lashing, leaving the room silent and awkward.

Those were the first words I ever said to my husband.

"His version—take two!"
—CHUCK

It was a beautiful spring day in Arizona. The temperature was probably a nice 75 degrees. The wind was lightly blowing outside, and I could hear footsteps coming toward the door. As I turned to see who it was, my breath was taken away. There was this gorgeous, enchanting woman coming through the door. As she brushed her platinum blonde hair to the side, she glanced in my direction, and I knew it was love at first sight.

Okay, actually, I don't think she even looked my way.

I was staring at her voluptuous body as she walked by in her tan pants and red shirt and sat down near the front of the room. My day, all of a sudden, got better.

I looked up at the front of the room and the husband team leader was laughing, knowing I would have that reaction. I silently asked, "Who is that?" and the husband team leader shrugged me off, mouthing, "I'll tell you later."

So, as the team meeting started, I sat in the back, once again with no contribution to give to the meeting. As usual, the wife team leader would gather all the sales and listings from the team and write them on the board.

Now, I knew the team leaders. I was friends with them and we would hang out outside of work. I had actually spent time at their home and knew their family, so I felt like I could say whatever I wanted, as a friend. The wife team leader must have been on a diet. She had lost some weight.

As she was putting sales on the board, I emphatically yelled out, "Hey, are you on a diet?"

She turned around with a big smile on her face and said, "Why yes, Chuck, I am. Can you tell?"

I answered, "Yes. I can see the board now." Now mind you, to me, that was a compliment, but not according to this beautiful blonde girl, whom I had set eyes on for the very first time that day.

She turned around and from this beautiful mouth comes a roar of words I will never forget—the words from the future love of my life, "What are you, an a$$h@!e?"

What a surprise! How could such a girl think of me that way? I was a charming young lad! Well, not really. But, the tongue lashing . . . anyway, those were the words first spoken by my future wife. Under my breath, this brash New Yorker has some choice words for her too . . .

That's okay. I let it roll off my back. I said to myself, "She just does not yet know how charming I am."

I will still defend myself to this day that I did not say that to the wife team leader in a negative way. It really was a compliment.

"How Chuck went from just some a$$h@!e to the love of my life . . . "
—ANGELA

So, how did we move from our intense first encounter to future soulmates?

I'll have to give you the reader's digest version. Chuck did try to pursue me a bit but, in my ignorance, I just didn't think he was my type. I'll expose myself even more by admitting that I assumed he was dumb. He was good looking and brash sounding, which didn't seem to go with smart. (Who's the dumb one?)

There was a day that I was looking all around the real estate office for someone to go and have a beer with me. All the girls were busy. I walked into another part of the office, still determined, and whom do I see? Chuck was sitting at one of the computers. I remember that I actually rolled my eyes, but I really wanted a beer. I asked him to join me, and we went across the street to a local place. We spent the whole time having a debate. It didn't go well, and I am not sure I even appreciated my beer.

Time passed and I was still really new to real estate and new to the things that go along with real estate, such as checking my email, phone and pager on a regular basis for messages. One day,

I finally checked my pager messages and found a sweet message from Chuck that he had left several days earlier. I wasn't interested in him, but I immediately felt like an idiot because I'm sure it seemed like I totally ignored him. I called him to apologize for overlooking his message, and we ended up going out. We initially met in March and officially started dating sometime in June. In August, he showed up at my door with a toothbrush, and the rest is history.

CHAPTER TWO

DO YOU *REALLY* WANT TO BE IN REAL ESTATE?

f you interviewed 1,000 kids and asked them what they want to be when they grow up, you'd probably get the following answers:

- Princess

- Fireman

- Football player (or other sports player)

- Doctor

- Teacher

- Monster truck driver

- Policeman

- Builder

11

I asked a bunch of kids myself, and the most interesting answer I got was "special effects make-up artist." That kid was a teenager. In fact, the older the kid, the more sophisticated or specific the answers were. We also heard "computer science engineer" and "author."

Funny thing is, no matter how many kids we asked, guess what didn't make the list?

Real estate agent.

I personally don't know anyone who told me that, from as far back as they could remember, they wanted to be a real estate agent. Out of all of our six kids, we've never found them playing "real estate." They've played school, restaurant, hotel, MMA smack down, fashion show, dance party, master fort builders . . . but not real estate.

Neither Chuck nor I ever had the aspiration to become real estate agents. When I was in my early twenties, I was dating someone who had a real estate license and who convinced me that I should get my license. I actually went to most of the classes and just never finished. I wasn't interested at all!

Our kids, even being around us as successful agents, don't want to be in real estate. Our two oldest, Danielle and Charles, were with us a lot when they were young. They would go on appointments and spend time with us when we prospected. By the time Danielle was a teenager, she could have run circles around most agents. However, neither one of them had a desire to be in real estate.

So, why do people get into real estate? Here are some of the reasons we've heard:

- I lost my job and wasn't sure what else to do.

- I've stayed at home for so long, and now I want to get out in the real world.

- I have no other options.

- The kids are all out of the house.

- I've always loved looking at houses.

- I want to be my own boss.

- I want to do something that can make me a lot of money.

The funny thing is, none of those reasons has anything to do with the actual process of making it in real estate. Are any of these reasons (or something similar) yours? Regardless of the reason people get into real estate, most want to be successful at it. We have spoken with thousands of agents who tell us that they want to be a successful real estate agent. The statistics of success in our industry, however, do not match up with how many people say they desire success. In 2012, the Texas Association of REALTORS® conducted a web survey through Zoomerang. The survey went out to 13,000 broker/manager members and one of the purposes was to try to identify why new agents fail. They identified four areas:

1. Lack of adequate startup capital—Simply put, they didn't have enough money. They didn't anticipate the start-up fees, cost of materials and the time it takes to get going in the business with no incoming dollars.

2. Unrealistic expectations—We know this is true for sure. Many new agents think real estate will be this never-ending,

fun episode of HGTV's "House Hunters." The reality of how hard it is hits about month three. Furthermore, most new agents don't realize that they're not entering into a "job," but rather a sales business. That's a big shocker for most.

3. Part-time vs. full-time—We have known *very* few agents who have successfully built a career as a part-time agent. Being a top notch, successful REALTOR® demands full-time hours (or more).

4. Mindset—We will spend quite a bit of time on this one. Mindset is, in our opinion, the number-one killer of the new agent.

The Truth: How Much Money it Really Takes to Get Started in Real Estate

One of the most mind-blowing realizations that many new real estate agents come to is that starting their business costs money *and* they won't probably make money right away. I don't know why this is such a surprise. Even the IRS recognizes that most new businesses don't make money in their first couple of years. Logically, it only makes sense that a new business will require capital and that it will take time to build. Somehow, though, agent after agent thinks they will start their real estate business with little or no out-of-pocket expense and that they should have plenty of closings in the first couple of months to start paying all their bills with money left over to plan that dream vacation. They've hardly started, and they're already taking time off in their minds.

New agents need money for their dues and fees, business cards, signs and basic materials, at the very least. In addition, many agents find it off-putting or even offensive that their brokerage is not a non-profit organization. The truth is that if agents do all they are supposed to do in terms of prospecting and follow up in an intense way, they might start closing deals within the first three to four months. Therefore, agents need this crazy thing called cash reserves to live and pay their bills while they work hard to get started.

What fees are needed to get started? Of course, it varies from state to state, but everyone will have the same categories of start-up costs. There is a cost to the licensing process. Usually the schooling and testing portion will be less than $1000. Once you are licensed, you will have fees to join your local real estate board, and there are fees to join a brokerage. In the Phoenix metro area, your real estate start-up fees equates to about $1000. Your business cards, signs and basic materials will run you $500 to $1000. We recommend that you have from $2500 to $3000 available to invest in these basic start-up fees.

If you are not yet in real estate and decide that you will pursue this career, we also recommend that you have a good four to five months of reserves. That means you'd better start skipping Starbucks and buy some rice, beans and pasta. Being financially prepared can mean the difference between success and failure.

Unrealistic Expectations (and What You SHOULD Expect)

New agents have all kinds of unrealistic expectations, including:

- I don't need much training.

- There's no need to learn scripts.

- I shouldn't have to prospect that much to find business.

- All my friends and family will use me to buy and sell.

- I don't mix business with friends and family.

- It's more important to save money than to pay a great brokerage for their tools, systems, training and support.

- I'll make money fast.

- I can manage my own schedule.

- I'm super accountable on my own.

- I sat an open house once, and it didn't work.

We could go on and on.

Here's the truth for all you readers that have unrealistic expectations (and no, you're not the exception):

- You need training, and you should learn scripts.

- Prospecting will consume much of your time in the first few years if you want to succeed.

- If you don't give your friends and family a reason to trust you as a good REALTOR®, they might not use you.

- You'd better mix business with *everything*!

- A great brokerage can *hugely* impact your ability to succeed.

- It's more important to make money than to save it.

- You won't necessarily make money fast.

- You're probably not that accountable.

- *Yes*, open houses work!

Having the right expectations can make all the difference in the world for a new agent.

Unfortunately, our experience is that real estate agents have far more influences around them that feed into unrealistic expectations than influences that speak the truth boldly to them. We have always been passionate about shooting straight with agents. The success of our agents manifests into the success of our business. Agents are our clients and we serve them heartily unto the Lord. Part of doing this properly involves communicating the right expectations.

If you were able to interview a sampling of our agents that are involved in our brokerage, you would hear some similar statements. You'd hear we're intense and passionate about the business and their success. They would say that we are super hands on, and you would definitely hear that we tell it like it is. We constantly remind our agents about the right expectations they should have about this business. Whether they really hear it or not is another question.

As an aside, nobody ever said that we like sitting in someone else's home for six hours or that we like knocking on strangers' doors. We don't generally like calling random people or driving people we don't know around for hours (or days) on end. However, we understand that these activities are part of embracing the process in order to become successful.

Part-time vs. Full-time (a.k.a. Why Part-Time Agents Almost Always Fail)

When we refer to part-time agents, we are generally talking about agents that have another job. These agents think that they can get a real estate business off the ground on evenings and weekends. The only part-time agents we have ever known to succeed were those with a definite plan to quit their job, and then they put in an incredible amount of effort on their off times to make it happen. The success rate is exceedingly low.

There's another type of "part-time." They disguise themselves as full-time REALTORS®. They don't have another job, but, when exposed, it's obvious that they work part-time. They're only kidding themselves when they call themselves full-time. Chuck and I often say, "If you were your own boss, would you have fired yourself already?" Most of these agents fail, too.

How are these stealthy part-time agents exposed? They simply aren't productive. The great thing about real estate is that if you do the proper activities, build your skills and have the right mindset, you'll make money. So, when an agent is not productive, it's a tell-tale sign that they probably only work part-time.

Chuck loves to sit down with agents who claim they are working hard but aren't making money. He is a *master* at this type of a meeting. There are several characteristics my sweet husband has that causes him to be so good at this. First, his discernment about people is off the charts. I have learned (as have many of our closest friends and family) that when Chuck has a gut feeling about someone, it's almost always spot on.

Secondly, he has an uncanny gift of questioning. Many people shy away from confrontation. Chuck doesn't. But while most people who aren't afraid to confront will ask questions to try to get to the bottom of something, Chuck will not just ask questions. He will drill down and drill down and drill down until he gets to the root. Double-talking him never, ever works, and he can read people like a book.

It is with pure skill that Chuck navigates through these meetings with agents. It starts with the agents saying something like they work hard but aren't getting anywhere. It almost always ends up with Chuck exposing their schedule as that of part-time agents with little or no intensity in purpose, direction or structure.

Chuck and Angela's definition of full time: You work at least forty hours per week, and 50-60% of your time is spent in the following activities:

- Prospecting
- Follow up
- Appointments
- Listing homes
- Writing purchase contracts
- Closing homes

There's a lot more to success than just this, but if you can truly describe your schedule as conforming to this definition, you are on your way to success and you are, in fact, full time.

By the way, *great news*: there is a level of success that you can achieve in real estate where you don't always have to work forty hours per week! It just takes a whole bunch of effort and a lot of time to get there.

3 Questions that Can Determine if You Have the Right Mindset to Succeed

Much of this book concerns mindset. That includes seeing real estate as it really is, getting the right perspective of how to achieve success, exposing bad mindsets and giving strategies to achieve the right mindset. We'll address more concerning mindset in later chapters.

But first, ask yourself these three crucial questions to determine if your mindset is in the right place:

1. *Are you prepared financially to start a career in real estate?*

2. *Are you willing to put forth the time and effort it takes to succeed?*

3. *Do you believe you have reasonable expectations of what it will take to be a real estate agent?*

CHAPTER THREE

DISCOVER IF REAL ESTATE IS YOUR IDEAL CAREER

Tell Me What You Want (What You Really, Really Want)

Mark Manson wrote an article entitled, *The Most Important Question of Your Life.* The introductory words were:

> Everybody wants what feels good. Everyone wants to live a carefree, happy and easy life, to fall in love and have amazing sex and relationships, to look perfect and make money and be popular and well-respected and admired and a total baller to the point that people part like the Red Sea when you walk into the room.
>
> Everyone would like that — it's easy to like that.

21

If I ask you, "What do you want out of life?" and you say something like, "I want to be happy and have a great family and a job I like," it's so ubiquitous that it doesn't even mean anything.

A more interesting question, a question that perhaps you've never considered before, is what pain do you want in your life? What are you willing to struggle for? Because that seems to be a greater determinant of how our lives turn out.

———

What pain do you want in your life? That's his question. We think that's a darn good question.

If I just asked you that question without any context, many of you would answer, "None!"

When you look at this question more closely, I'm not sure you'll ultimately say that you don't want any pain. First, let's start with what people typically say they want:

- An amazing job
- Financial independence
- Awesome relationships
- That incredible car
- A beautiful house
- A rockin' body

The list can be long and diverse. Does everyone get what they say they want? Of course not! Let's take the example of wanting an awesome relationship. An over 50% divorce rate will testify to the fact that we don't always get what we say we want. How could this happen? How can you want a happy marriage, say "I do," and then end up divorcing? The question is, did you *really* want that happy marriage?

Getting what you want requires struggle.

There are so many ways that we are all the same. One universal similarity is that experiencing positive things is easy to handle . . . at least at first. I think we would all agree that if you have your eye on that certain guy or girl, and they like you back, that feels super easy at first. If you want that promotion and then you are granted it, it feels great . . . at least at first. An initial win feels amazing.

However, it's the negative experiences that we struggle with right from the beginning.

What we get out of life is determined not only by the good experiences but also by which bad things, negative experiences and struggles we're willing and able to tough our way through so that we can get to the successes.

Here are some examples:

1. Most people can't have an amazing body without appreciating the pain and physical stress of exercise or calculating all that you eat.

2. Owning your own business or becoming financially independent doesn't usually happen without taking risks, failing a lot, and working many hours—all without knowing if you will ultimately be successful.

3. You don't end up attracting someone amazing in a relationship without going through trials, rejections, hard conversations and compromise.

Plenty of people think they want something, but what does it mean to really want something?

Wanting something means not only wanting the benefits or the end result. It is also wanting the process that goes along with it. For example:

1. You say you want to lose weight, gain a strong body, etc. Do you really want that? Do you want to:

    a. Exercise—I mean, *really*? Are you committed to exercising on a regular basis? Pushing your body? Maybe getting up early?

    b. Eat right—Are you ready to skip that dessert? Change your eating habits? Feel hungry?

2. Or how about your goal of making a lot of money in real estate? Do you want to:

    a. Prospect and constantly meet new people?

    b. Create systems and organization to keep in touch with prospects and maintain your client database?

    c. Spend time learning your contracts?

    d. Practice scripts? And the list goes on.

Mr. Manson is right on the money about the idea of wanting something. He explains that if you think you want something and time goes by—weeks, months, years—and you are no closer to the end result, maybe what you actually want is just a fantasy or a day dream. Maybe you just enjoy wanting. Maybe you don't really want it at all.

The One Question that Can Change Your Life

Mark Manson wrote that he likes to ask people this question: *"How do you choose to suffer?"*

He believes the answer to that question can change your life. The answer is what defines us.

He gave an example from his own life. Here's what he said:

> For most of my adolescence and young adulthood, I fantasized about being a musician — a rock star, in particular. Any badass guitar song I heard, I would always close my eyes and envision myself up on stage playing it to the screams of the crowd, people absolutely losing their minds to my sweet finger-noodling. This fantasy could keep me occupied for hours on end. The fantasizing continued up through college, even after I dropped out of music school and stopped playing seriously. But even then it was never a question of if I'd ever be up playing in front of screaming crowds, but when. I was biding my time before I could invest the proper amount of time and effort into getting out there and making it work. First, I needed to finish school. Then, I needed to make money. Then, I needed to find the time. Then… and then nothing.
>
> Despite fantasizing about this for over half of my life, the reality never came. And it took me a long time and a lot of negative experiences to finally figure out why: I didn't actually want it.
>
> I was in love with the result — the image of me on stage, people cheering, me rocking out, pouring my heart into what I'm playing — but I wasn't in love

with the process. And because of that, I failed at it. Repeatedly. Hell, I didn't even try hard enough to fail at it. I hardly tried at all.

———

He said that he wanted the reward and not the struggle. He wanted the result and not the process.

Sure, he wanted to be a famous rock star but he did not want the acts of:

- Lugging around equipment

- Rehearsing

- Working to get a record deal

- Getting people to show up and watch him

He said, "I was in love NOT with the fight, but only the victory and life doesn't work that way."

To further illustrate this point, Chuck and I both like Mixed Martial Arts (MMA). He actually watches it more than I do, but I think I imagine myself in the ring more than he does. Really, I do. I love to work out, and I imagine that I would love to be an MMA fighter. Keep in mind, I don't really *want* to do this. I don't want to get hit in the face, and I don't want a lot of bruises. I have also heard that broken bones hurt quite a bit. However, in my mind, I'm an awesome fighter.

That's an obnoxious example, I know, but many people *want* to be agents in the same way I want to be an MMA fighter.

How to Identify What You Truly Want in Life

Ultimately, what you really want has some characteristics: You not only want the end result, but you want the struggles and pain that come along with the process it takes to get to the end result.

We ask people often, "Why do you want to get into real estate?" We get answers like:

- I love to show homes!

- I just don't want to be in the corporate world anymore!

- I want freedom of time.

- I have bought and sold myself several times, and it's fun.

No one has EVER said to us, "I love to meet new people! In fact, I can't wait to call strangers up on the phone, knock on the doors of people I've never met, and ask all my friends and family for business! Can't wait to learn all of these contracts and see how fun will it be to do all that paperwork!"

Well, we wouldn't expect that. However, if we follow up with questions like:

- How do you feel about knocking on stranger's doors?

- Do you like to meet new people?

- Are you excited to learn how to make phone calls to get clients?

- . . . sometimes the answers reveal that maybe they really don't want to make real estate their career.

You cannot truly want to be a successful agent without also wanting to have success in the process. It is highly unlikely that someone will enjoy great success in real estate if they don't want to prospect, follow up or ask people they know for business.

The great news is, I didn't say you have to love every step of the process. You can actually decide that you want to do something you don't love to do. I guarantee that super successful agents don't always love every part of being a real estate agent. However, they want the success so badly that they choose to want to do those things they don't love—and they choose it over and over again. They have discipline.

To help determine if you truly want real estate as your career, honestly answer these questions:

1. *Have you ever thought you wanted something just to find out you really don't?*

2. *Have you considered if you really want to be in real estate?*

3. *Are you prepared to prospect for your business?*

CHAPTER FOUR

HOW TO CHOOSE THE RIGHT BROKERAGE

When Chuck was first getting into real estate, he started considering the different companies that he could work for once he was licensed. One day he walked into one of those companies and had an interview. From his perception, everything seemed to go well and at the end of the interview, the guy he was talking to agreed to hire him. Chuck was *so excited*! He didn't even have his license yet, and already he had a job! He rushed to tell his dad the great news. Wow! Chuck felt special. Who could get offered a job before even being licensed?

Almost everyone.

The truth is, if you fog a mirror, most real estate brokerages will hire you. Although it's the norm, this is not universally true.

At our company, you are actually interviewing. That means that our recruiters are looking for certain qualities in potential agents and *yes*, we do turn people away. However, like I said, most brokerages will hire you—regardless of who you are—just as long as you will pay their fees and have a license.

The implication of this truth is that you have a choice of where you will work once you are licensed, and you should choose very, very carefully. *It matters where you hang your license!* How do you choose? There are several things to consider. First of all, you don't want to reinvent the wheel.

How to Avoid Reinventing the Wheel and Get the Support You Need to Succeed

When someone wants to become a teacher at an established school, they have to have a degree. That means they go to school and learn how to teach. Before teachers can actually graduate with their degree, they have to go through a process called student teaching. It usually starts out where the student is observing and assisting an established, experienced teacher. Throughout the process, the student teachers take on more and more responsibility until they are the ones teaching and the expert teacher is observing. This effective process helps teachers-to-be learn to handle a classroom on their own. Even when students become teachers, there is constant, on-going training throughout their careers to improve their craft.

The same idea is applied universally to doctors, policemen, firemen, lawyers, mechanics, technicians . . . almost every skilled career. What happens for most REALTORS®? They have to go through *one* licensing process. In Arizona, it's only ninety hours of classroom work and then a couple of tests to pass. I don't know that it's true in every state, but in all of them that I know about, the licensing training isn't practical to the actual career at all! You are learning information simply to pass the test and most of it you'll never use in the day-to-day practice of real estate. It's kind of sad when the big joke in real estate school is that they are just taught to pass the test.

Once licensed, there is no requirement at all to go through any additional training, except to take renewal hours for your state's real estate department. Most of those classes are not applicable to the day-to-day practice of being an agent either. Overall, there is no requirement to get mentorship, practical training or anything similar. What I'm saying is, anyone can get a license and then practice real estate the next day after being licensed. Considering that a person's house is usually the single most expensive item anyone will buy or sell in their life, this is frightening!

Thankfully, there are ways to get the support and resources you need to thrive as a successful real estate agent, starting with choosing the right brokerage. When you get your license, you have to hang it with a brokerage. At that brokerage, there is a designated broker. That person's responsibility is to oversee their agents. You would think, then, that the brokerage level is where agents receive their practical training and mentorship. By and large, brokerages fail miserably at this task.

There are definitely exceptions! I know of companies that offer excellent mentorship and training programs. However, this is not required industry wide and FAR more agents join brokerages that don't train well than those who find a supportive, effective brokerage. When you are interviewing brokerages, one of your criteria must be that they offer practical, quality training that will shorten your learning curve.

Crucial Questions to Ask Before Choosing a Brokerage

Here is the challenge: Many brokerages proclaim to have amazing training. How will you know if it's true? There are several ways to investigate so that you can get a measure of the truth.

First of all, anytime you interview with a brokerage, you will want a copy of their roster. That way, you will be able to call any of their current agents to ask them a series of questions.

Secondly, ask the person interviewing you, "Who are your instructors? Have they ever sold real estate? If so, how much have they sold?" Get a bio of the instructor(s). Sadly, many instructors never experienced any success at all. How can they coach you to success if they never experienced it for themselves? Chuck and I are two of the primary instructors. We have other instructors, and every one of them that teaches about the foundational principles of success in a real estate career has vast experience and success. That's what you're looking for in a training program.

Chuck says:

> I think it's ridiculous that for ninety hours (which is what you need in Arizona to get a real estate license) you can be licensed to sell somebody's biggest asset of their entire life. Don't get me started about the fact that there's actually a crash course to ram all this information down your throat in a very short amount of time. Getting a license to cut hair is actually more expensive, takes a longer time and has more extensive classroom work. Now, what about the cost of getting a license? It is far less expensive to get into the profession of real estate than to get into most other professions or businesses. Many real estate instructors would even tell you that most of the stuff they teach

in class pertains only to helping you pass the test and that most of it isn't relevant or practical to what you need in your career. If we raise the cost and the time frame, it would weed out a lot of the people who are not serious about this profession. These unprofessional agents give us professionals a bad rap. That is why at our brokerage, we have different standards than the minimum this industry conforms agents to.

I believe this industry is incredibly broken. Besides what it takes to get into the business, let's talk about how easy and inexpensive it is to keep your license. I don't know how it is in other states, but in Arizona, all agents have to do to keep their licenses is take 24 hours of renewal credits every two years. That would be great if the choice of classes actually helped agents grow. However, the truth is, all agents have to do is sit through a class that's probably irrelevant to helping them become better or worse agents, or sit online and almost mindlessly click through a series of boxes answering questions. This happens every two years, and they keep their license.

Most real estate brokerages, in general, do little or nothing to contribute to helping an agent be professional. How sad is it that a company can have hundreds or thousands of agents—having no idea who they are—and provide little more than a place to hang their licenses to the detriment of other professional agents who have to interact with them along with the general public, who have no idea who's really representing them. Probably one of the saddest things of all is that agents can get their broker's license (at least in Arizona) with no more credentials than being in the business for three years. All they have to do is take *the same* classes they took to get

33

their original license, plus nine hours of broker-specific content. Then they pass a test. It has nothing to do with production or their level of expertise. In fact, there are lots of brokers who become managing or designated brokers of companies that we personally know could never make it in the business so they got their broker's license in order to get a JOB to help other agents be successful. That's frightening.

It's one of the reasons why our company, Revelation Real Estate, has a level of standards that is different than the industry norm.

We had no Master Oogway—no Mr. Miyagi

In case you haven't seen the animated Kung Fu Panda movies, Master Oogway is an elderly tortoise that is credited with being the creator of kung fu and developer of the Dragon Warrior legend. He was known for his wisdom, knowledge and experience, and he shared all of this with his pupils. He helped people . . . well, not really. He helped a tiger, a crane, a praying mantis, a viper, a monkey and, yes, a panda.

Mr. Miyagi is one of the lead characters in the movie *Karate Kid*. He is an unassuming handyman who, oh by the way, happens to be a master of martial arts. He befriends the other main character, Daniel, who is the new kid in town. Daniel is getting bullied, so Mr. Miyagi trains him to be this amazing martial artist and, of course, he competes and wins against the brutal Cobra Kai.

When we say, we had no Master Oogway—no Mr. Miyagi, we simply mean that we, like many real estate agents, had nobody to "show us the way" in this career.

However, that really isn't a good excuse. As a result of the overall failure of brokerages to train their agents, many different training and coaching companies have risen up over the years. Agents have many opportunities to seek out good training on their own. We **didn't** seek out training, and that was dumb.

At first, we were failures in the business. We, theoretically, shouldn't have failed. We were at a company that brags about their training, and we were on a team that was supposed to help and guide us. Seriously, we were paying over 50% of our commissions, and in exchange for what? We were willing workers, eager and hungry and not at all lazy. We're not generalizing that this was the experience of every agent at this particular company (in case you know what it was). We're just saying that our particular office and our particular team were not effective.

After about six months of working together and getting more broke all the time, the Lord sent us a messenger. Her name was Donna, and here's how it happened. Chuck and I were sitting in our office. I use the word "office" very loosely. It was actually a utility closet that the team leaders let us clear out and move into. It was literally no more than 5' x 8' of space.

So, we're sitting in our office, and Donna, one of our teammates, walks by. She stuck her head into our office to say hi. "Rumor has it you're leaving!" announces my blunt husband. Donna proceeded to tell us about her impending move. The Lord started a little whisper into our hearts. We started praying about whether or not we should consider a move.

We decided to check out a couple of other brokerages and what they offer. We chose an office. Truth be told, there really wasn't anything much appealing about the office we checked out, except the fees. But seriously, we didn't come across another brokerage that offered anything compelling, so why not choose based on fees? We felt nudged by the Lord for sure that we were supposed to leave.

In fact, in the few days after we decided we would be moving, a couple of the girls who were our teammates wanted to leave with us and be a part of our team.

Our team? Didn't they know that we were completely broke and had no clue? We even told them these very obvious facts. They still wanted to come and *poof*, we were team leaders.

I'd like to say we had an amazing time at our going-away party that our team leaders threw for us. Many of the agents in the company showed up to wish us well, including the owner.

Ha! I don't think so. In fact, the owner gave us an inspiring going-away speech by telling us that we were going to fail and everyone we brought with us would fail. Now, why would the owner care at all about a couple of peons like us? We were just shy of the last nail in the coffin of our real estate career. Chuck believes that maybe the Lord allowed the owner to speak these words knowing that they would be fuel in future months and years to keep us pressing forward. One thing I can tell you for sure is you should never give my sweet husband a challenge if you won't want to see him succeed. His competitive spirit is off the charts. Nevertheless, Chuck, Nina, Michelle and I moved on to our new office. That was January, 2002.

The first day we walked into the Ahwatukee office as their new agents, Chuck saw a plaque on the wall next to the front desk. On that plaque were the names of the number one agents in the company for several years past. Chuck pointed to that plaque and proclaimed boldly to the office manager, "I'm going to be your number one agent." I have a terrible memory, but I probably thought something like, "Is this man sane? Am I?"

At the time, this brokerage had about 3500 agents. Keep in mind that we had no money and no plan. The brokerage offered no training, no mentorship and no coaching. It was a "you're on your own, pay us our fees" company, and that's all. We had no Master Oogway—no Mr. Miyagi. We were completely on our own, except for the mighty grace of God.

We Reinvented the Wheel (and Unnecessarily Wasted Time, Money & Energy)

Instead of studying how other successful people had prospected, we tried different things until they worked. Over time, we would catch wind of one idea or another, and we would implement those things into our business. Sometimes they worked, but many times they didn't. It was painful and unnecessary.

"But you made it!" you say. It's true, but we wasted a lot of time and money getting there.

One year, when we were agents and making some money, a news station approached us about being their exclusive agents. We thought it was the opportunity of a lifetime. We took a huge risk and paid $36,000 to accept their offer, thinking that it would only take five or six closings to cover the cost. Obviously, we imagined that this popular news station could attract many quality leads.

To be fair, we definitely got a quantity of leads—lots and lots of leads mostly looking to buy homes really far from where we worked. Chuck and I spent so much time scrubbing each of these leads, and at the end of the year we closed exactly one deal. *One!* Looking back, if we had not tried to reinvent the wheel, we would have known that this type of an offering would never work. We made many of these types of mistakes and yes, we did put our faces on a bench in front of a supermarket. That didn't work either.

This same problem causes many real estate agents to suffer in their businesses as well. Quite simply, agents don't know how to build their businesses in a thoughtful and effective way. In order to avoid this "reinventing of the wheel," agents should carefully consider who they align themselves with in their career, including their brokerage and the other professionals they choose to surround themselves with.

Lesson: You don't have to re-invent the wheel in real estate. It's really hard to do so, and it wastes time, money and energy. Find a brokerage, a mentor or a team leader that shortens your learning curve. It's worth whatever you have to pay! Just beware: Many companies will try to sell you into believing they are the best. Be careful with your choice!

We've already mentioned that you need to join a brokerage (or team within a brokerage or a mentorship program) that offers high-quality, practical training. Another element you *must* look for is broker support. The role of a great broker is to be there for their agents. The same rule of thumb applies to the litmus test for brokers as it does for the people training you. Your broker should have the experience to not only know the contracts in and out but also have the experience to help you in practical application. There are brokers out there in charge of agents and their professional development that have sold almost no homes at all. So, you're putting your real estate career in the hands of someone who may have never even made it in real estate themselves.

At our brokerage, we currently have six brokers on staff. All of them have practical real estate experience, and four of them were top producers. We know the business, and we can advise our agents in an excellent way. *You need that!* Do not join a brokerage where your broker is inexperienced in the practical application of real estate or totally disengaged with the day-to-day operations of a brokerage.

When we started our brokerage, we were really clear on a couple of things:

- We did *not* want our agents to have to reinvent the wheel. It's not necessary, and it's super painful! Therefore, our agents have access to some of the industry's best training, mentorship, tools and systems.

- We fully believe that whom you surround yourself with affects your business, so we have dedicated ourselves to building and improving on a culture conducive to success.

- Passionate leadership is infectious! We lead with passion and excellence, and it rubs off on people around us.

Are you thoughtfully considering these things as you embark on your real estate career? If you're not yet in real estate, make sure you interview carefully when choosing a brokerage. Don't just interview and decide. Emotions can run high during this selection process. Call the existing agents and ask them all types of questions to be sure that you're making the right choice. If you're already in real estate and you've realized you're in the wrong place, *move*—and quickly!

At the end of this chapter, and again at the end of the book, we have listed some great interview questions for you to use when searching for the right place to work. In many of the following chapters, we discuss things to seek out and things to avoid in real estate. Our intention is to set you on the path to success and to learn how to not reinvent the wheel.

Before we move on, ask yourself:

1. *Do you really believe that it is crucial to have great training?*

2. *Are you prepared to be a life-long learner?*

3. *Will you pursue the type of brokerage that can help you in your career?*

Brokerage interview questions:

1. What type of training can I expect to receive?

2. Do you have a mentorship program? If yes, what does it entail? Who are your mentors and what success have they experienced in real estate?

3. Who are the instructors? What makes them qualified to teach those courses? What success have they experienced in real estate?

4. Is there a training class I could sit in on before making a decision about your brokerage?

5. Who are the brokers? What success have they experienced in real estate? How accessible are the brokers? How do I reach them?

6. How does your brokerage keep agents informed about the industry and the market?

7. May I have a copy of your agent roster so that I can ask some of them questions about what it's like to work here?

8. What tools and systems do you offer?

CHAPTER FIVE

MAP YOUR SUCCESS

We have to start this chapter with the assumption that you want good things out of life. You may be clear on exactly what you want, or perhaps you haven't taken the time to articulate what you're after. However, one thing is certain: If you want to have a successful career in real estate, you'd better have a map.

Most people would never take a road trip to somewhere they've never been without the trip mapped out. That would be a terrible idea, unless you don't care where you end up. The same is true for your life. You have a choice. One option is just go day to day and see where life takes you. That's perfectly fine if you don't care where you end up. Chances are, you do care, and even if you're not absolutely sure of where you want to be in your life, you will have a much better chance of arriving somewhere pleasant if you have a plan.

There are volumes of information about goal setting, vision boards and your "big why." Research definitively concludes that the process of goal setting, getting clear on your vision and identifying your "big why" contributes significantly to achievement. You must do these things. You must have a plan.

How to Put Your Subconscious to Work Finding Opportunities

I love Google. I use it all the time. In fact, Chuck and I marvel about the ability to grab information so easily and quickly. Our family can be in the car, and a question can be posed. Within seconds, someone is either Googling it or asking Siri.

I prefer Google. Siri can really be difficult sometimes. Sure, she sounds nice . . . but I digress.

I conclude that I love Google because writing this book has caused my reticular activating system to notice how often I Google things. In case you're not familiar, a reticular activating system can be described as a part of the brain that stays alert. Your brain filters through all the information and stimuli around you. If you actually noticed every single sound and sight around you without the filter, your brain would be on overload, and you couldn't focus on anything. So, your brain pays attention to some things but ignores others.

Another example is that when you buy (or want to buy) a new car, suddenly you notice how many of that type of car are all around you. There are so many! (Except you ridiculously wealthy people who buy a Bugatti Veyron Super Sports . . . Google it). Or maybe you're pregnant and all of a sudden there are pregnant ladies everywhere you go. It's your brain altering its filters to pay attention to different parts of your environment.

Information about the reticular activating system can be useful to REALTORS®, particularly in the area of goal setting. We have all heard the importance of goal setting. People say things like, "How can you know where you're going if you don't map out the way?" That's certainly true, but there's even more power associated with goal setting in real estate.

One Simple Trick to Prime Your Brain for Reaching Your Goals

Goal setting initiates your reticular activating system. You can strengthen the effects by writing these goals down and seriously speed track your results when you look at and read your goals regularly. Think about it this way: Let's say you have a goal of going on six listing appointments per month. You write down, "I will go on six appointments per month." You say to yourself every day before you prospect, "I will go on six appointments per month." You visualize yourself getting these appointments. You have actually primed your brain to look more intensely for opportunities to get listing appointments.

If you had not set this goal, perhaps you wouldn't pick up as readily on the verbal clues a person may give in an open house. This mistake certainly wouldn't be intentional. You simply did not prepare your brain properly to receive the clues and information. The opportunities are all around you. You need to train your brain to recognize them.

One of our good friends and an agent of ours, Nicole Stevens, just recently experienced great success with this concept. She shared a goal with me that she wanted to have $2.8 million of closed or in escrow business in a little over three months. She wrote her goal down. She said it out loud and then visualized it intently every day and sometimes several times a day. In the first week of seriously implementing this plan, Nicole put $1 million of business in escrow. That's just cool!

Tickle Your Brain

What should you do, then, knowing this powerful bit of information? Tickle your brain.

Make goals! Write them down! Review them every day and say them out loud before you prospect. In fact, you should consider writing down goals that have to do with the most important real estate activities you can do, which are:

- Prospecting
- Follow up
- Making appointments
- Writing contracts

Can you imagine if you had a goal that said, "I will follow up with my leads assertively and effectively every day to get appointments"? What might happen if you wrote it down and said it to yourself before your follow up time block each day? You will be amazed at the ideas and opportunities that show up when you train your mind to focus on achieving in each area that leads to money in real estate.

For example, we used to have a recruiter named Jon. Jon had no fear when it came to recruiting. Sometimes no filters either, but definitely no fear. He did a great job for a long time. We gave him recruiting goals, and our biggest push for him was to get to 300 agents. To make it fun, my husband likened his goal to the Spartan movie *300*. He even Photoshopped Jon's face on to the Spartan guy's face and posted it where Jon could regularly see it. Chuck and Jon shouted Spartan stuff at each other all the time. It was obnoxious, for sure, but it worked. Jon got us to the 300 agent milestone. That's the power of goal setting and visualization; it just works.

Tickle your brain every day, and laugh yourself all the way to the bank!

Two Concepts that Took Us from Broke to Funding a $75,000 Home Remodel in Just Three Months

When Chuck and I first started making money, we quickly realized the power of visualization and goal setting. There's something unbelievable about real estate, and it concerns your ability to earn money. Your efforts can directly affect your income.

To illustrate this point, we lived in an older house in Ahwatukee, which was Chuck's house before it was ours. I had a house that was smaller, and we decided that it was better used as a rental than Chuck's house. There was a small problem with Chuck's house: It was a total bachelor's pad. The carpet was grey. The walls were grey. Chuck's bed was a shiny grey lacquer (and yes, it had a mirror on it), and his curtains were black. The tile was grey too, and when you walked into that house, you just wanted to curl up into a little ball and cry.

To paint you an even better picture, there was a time when Chuck had every room in that house rented to a different person. Not only did he rent out every room but every *space*. There was a large hallway closet that someone rented out and the couch downstairs was rented out too, at $50 a month. This house was very, very special.

We both agreed that the home needed an overhaul. Furthermore, we wanted to put an addition onto the house because a friend of ours and her son needed a place to live. The renovation would cost about $75,000.

Seventy-five thousand dollars! Remember, just a few months before we were *totally broke*!

Chuck's a bigger thinker than I am sometimes. When we determined the cost, I thought it would take us about eight months to get there. This was in 2002, the very first year we made any money, and only a few months beyond our totally broke time. It was March or April when we decided to do the renovations. In my mind, eight months was an incredible goal.

But Chuck's impatient, and he thought eight months was too long to wait. We kicked up our intensity, and by June we had the money to do the remodel. June! That was only two or three months after we made our minds up that we wanted that money.

Looking back, I just don't know how to describe that experience. It opened my mind and Chuck's, too. That's when we realized that we can affect our own income. Real estate is amazing. You should work hard and get what you want.

Chuck says:

> Focusing your attention on something really big can change everything. This was true for us when we were super broke and had just switched brokerages after having five deals fall out of escrow. We were in the lobby of our new office, getting ready to start the next chapter of real estate. As we were waiting there, I saw a plaque with all the top-producing agents in that company year after year. There were 3500 agents at that company at the time. Remember, we were completely broke! I said, right out loud, "We will be on that plaque as the top-producing agent." To me, it

wasn't a wish; it was a vision that constantly repeated in my mind. Needless to say, we hit that goal more than once.

———

What about you?

1. *Are you willing to take the time to have written goals?*

2. *Have you considered what you hope to accomplish in real estate?*

3. *Are you excited about the opportunity to affect your own income?*

CHAPTER SIX

GET WORKING NOW

Once you are licensed, at a great brokerage and have a preliminary plan, it's time to get to work! You should be going through quality training, but you should also be working hard. What does that mean for a real estate agent? Whether you are new, struggling or trying to get to the next level, a large part of a real estate agent's work is prospecting. Before we get into prospecting details, we have a warning for you: Don't be a hotdog!

Are You a Hot Dog?

I'm somewhat of an anomaly, so I've been told. I have never had a Big Mac, Fillet of Fish, Quarter Pounder, Coke, thick shake, sundae or apple pie . . . nothing other than maybe a fry or two.

I have never eaten a meal from Burger King, Arby's, Wendy's or many other fast food restaurants. If they have a salad, I may have one of those minus the ooey, gooey packet of gross dressing. I just don't like fast food (except for that occasional fry). Therefore, the idea of a hot dog puts me over the edge! I get that hot dogs are this all-American food and that billions of hot dogs are consumed a year but really, do you know what they're made of?

A hot dog is composed from things that are inherently good: chicken, pork, and beef. However, if you take the worst part of chicken, pork and/or beef and mix it with a whole lot of other disgusting ingredients, you don't end up with something worth anything nutritionally.

I tried to find a hot dog enthusiast (go dogs, go!) article to defend the poor hot dog and found a post on huffingtonpost. com that was entitled, "In Defense of Hot Dogs, America's Most Underrated Meat." Although the article made several points about how vogue hot dogs are and how beginner chefs can't go wrong with hot dogs in their creations, when it comes to talking about the ingredients, the statements are less than enthusiastic:

*The meat they are made with isn't **that** mysterious.*

They're not the healthiest, but you can be an educated eater.

My conclusion is that a hot dog is a hot dog! It is made from dregs, which are, by definition, the least valuable part of anything.

Will it fill your stomach? Yes!

Will it seem like food? Yes!

Will it fill the time you're supposed to be eating? Yes!

But what are the true results from eating a hot dog? You're filling your body with junk, which is fine if you don't have any serious nutritional or physical goals. However, if you're looking to get in top physical shape, you're probably not going to fill your body with hot dogs. If weight loss is your goal, the hot dog is probably not on the diet. If you eat hot dogs every day, sooner or later you'll probably get sick or fat.

The Ingredients of a Top Agent

Why all this talk about hot dogs? What does this have to do with real estate?

It has everything to do with real estate. Our question to you is: Are *you* a hot dog?

To begin to answer this question, we need to discuss the "ingredients" of a great real estate agent. For the sake of this section, we'll talk about the actions of great agents.

These are the business-producing activities necessary to make money in real estate:

- Prospecting
- Follow up
- Appointments
- Listing homes
- Writing purchase contracts
- Closing homes

We'll focus on prospecting for a moment. Prospecting is the activity of seeking out people who are looking to buy or sell homes and are willing to allow you to help them. There are many ways to prospect. Some of them are:

- Holding open houses

- Door knocking

- Calling For Sale By Owners (FSBOs)

- Calling expired listings

All four of these examples of prospecting are "ingredients" that are good. They all work. However, if you take the dregs of prospecting and put them all together, you get a prospecting hot dog.

This is what agents will try: They'll do one open house for a couple of hours, putting two or three signs out; knock on doors one day with no compelling message, no script, and no call to action; contact an FSBO and a couple of expired listings and call it a week.

Maybe one day, agents will find someone who provides their information because they are thinking of buying a house. Agents wait three or four days before following up and leave a message asking for a phone call back. The phone call never comes, so they conclude that the prospect really wasn't looking to buy.

Agents may decide that they need some training so they go to one class, have some aha moments and then do nothing to act on what they heard.

Agents follow this type of schedule strictly for weeks and months and wonder why they aren't making any money.

These agents are hot dogs.

A hot dog agent takes a little bit of this and a little bit of that and does it halfway and half-heartedly. There's no intensity, no focus and no passion.

We will describe for you many examples of intensity, focus and passion as they pertain to a successful real estate career. Meanwhile, you need to ask yourself: *Am I a hot dog?*

Our Super Simple (Yet Supercharged) Prospecting and Follow-up Routine

When we first started in real estate, we didn't know that re-inventing the wheel was so difficult and costly. We also didn't know how much we would struggle unnecessarily, due both to a lack of proper leadership and lack of knowledge that we should have sought out mentorship. However, we were determined. We knew that we had to meet people.

What did we do?

- We sat open houses.

- We walked neighborhoods and apartment complexes and delivered 600-1000 fliers a week.

- We door knocked.

- We worked For Sale By Owners (FSBOs).

That's it. Oh, wait! I should also note that we did so in a super intense, "our lives depend upon it" way. When you are deciding what "super intense" is for you, keep this question in mind. How much time should you be prospecting? As a review, these are the business-producing activities necessary to make money in real estate:

- Prospecting

- Follow up

- Appointments
- Listing homes
- Writing purchase contracts
- Closing homes

Fifty to sixty percent of your time should be spent in these activities. For a forty-hour week, that would equate to at least twenty to twenty-five hours. When you're new or struggling, you probably don't have any appointments, listings, contracts or closings. That means twenty to twenty-five hours a week should be spent either prospecting or following up with potential clients. This commitment won't just happen naturally. You will have to be intentional with your time and intense in your efforts.

The Golden Tool that Took Us from Struggling to Thriving

That first year Chuck and I started making money, we used to door knock and deliver 600-1000 fliers every week. (No, "every week" is not a typo. Intensity, remember?) There was one tool that we used that year that was absolutely golden! We had heard about the idea of creating buyer books, which were informational tools we could give to potential buyers. Buyer books are filled with data concerning the buying process, including things such as inspections, title and escrow, lending, etc. Oftentimes, the book will also have utility information and moving checklists, along with the agent's contact information for when the buyer is ready to move forward.

We created a buyer book with the help from our escrow officer, Robbin, who was also a good friend of ours. Robbin was the closest thing we had to a mentor. Her family has a rich background in real estate, and she helped us all she could. Mostly, though, she just encouraged and pushed us to do more, always asking for more escrows.

The golden tool was not the buyer book itself but rather how we used it. At the time, we had a pager. (A what? For those of you who have no clue what I'm talking about, a pager is a rectangular, electronic device that receives messages and beeps or vibrates when a message is received.) In conjunction with the pager, we used our golden tool: Proquest. Proquest is a call capture system. You have a 1-800 number and codes. Then you develop ways to entice prospective clients to call the 1-800 number to hear recorded messages. We would get a pager message every time someone called our 800 number.

In 2002, there were several areas in the Phoenix metropolitan area where you could purchase brand-new homes for under $100K. Maricopa was one and lower Buckeye was another. There were others, but those were the two areas Chuck and I focused on. We took pictures of the fronts of the model homes and made fliers advertising skeletal information about these homes. It was enough information to be enticing, but not enough to know where to find them. We printed the 1-800 number along with corresponding codes for each home. On each flier we also offered the free buyer books we had.

During the time when we personally delivered 600-1000 fliers each week, many of those fliers went to apartment complexes. I was a complete chicken, and Chuck was like James Bond saving me from the menacing maintenance men on their golf carts, constantly trying to foil our efforts to thrive. It was actually really fun and great exercise. Chuck made me do most of the stairs because he has horrible knees. I loved the exercise! We made it a game.

And our pager went off *a lot*!

Where Most Agents Drop the Ball (and How to Set Yourself at the Top of the Pack)

Prospecting is essential. You have to meet people and find out if they are possible buyers or sellers and if they will work with you. However, you also need to know that prospecting is not where you will make most of your appointments. It's the follow up that will get you appointments. When following up, many agents drop the ball. They have a potential lead, and they call them maybe two or three times. If they haven't had success converting that lead, they give up.

That's too soon! *All* the research says so. Google it yourself. You should be following up at least fourteen to sixteen times before you begin to consider giving up. If you are going to follow up intensely—and you'd better if you want success— you need a system to keep track of your calls and reminders to follow up. Your amazing brokerage will have suggestions for you. Intense follow up must be placed into your regular schedule to ensure consistency.

Your Follow-Up Voicemail Script

A common question we get from newer agents is: When following up, should I leave a message, or just call back at a later time? Generally speaking, leave a message. However, you should leave the message in a very specific way to increase your chances of success.

For example:

> "Hello. This is Angela Fazio with Revelation Real Estate. I met you at the open house on Saturday and wanted to follow up with you. My number is 480-

555-5555, and you are free to call me if you'd like. However, I know you're busy, so I'll give you a call back on Wednesday afternoon."

Or:

"Hello. This is Angela Fazio with Revelation Real Estate. I see that you called about one of the properties on the flier I delivered to your house. My number is 480-555-5555, and you are free to call me if you'd like. However, I know you're busy, so I'll give you a call back on Wednesday afternoon."

The important elements of these messages are:

1. After identifying yourself, you remind them how you met them and/or why you're calling.

2. You give them your number spoken slowly so they have it if they want to call you.

3. You leave the responsibility for following up on you and *not* them.

4. You give them a timeframe of when you will call back.

Leaving the ball in your court for the follow-up is crucial. That way, there's not that awkwardness when you need to follow up with them again. If you ask them to call you back and they don't, you're more likely to not follow up, using the excuse that they aren't interested since they didn't call. That's not necessarily accurate. People are busy, or perhaps it's not their first priority at the moment.

Following up when you say you will is important, too. First of all, it shows the level of integrity you have, because you actually did what you said you were going to do. It also shows that you are organized and professional, which are two qualities people want in their agent. Finally, because each of your messages is friendly and non-confrontational, you are more likely to get them to either call you back eventually or answer when you call. They will appreciate your persistence or tell you to bug off. Either way, you'll succeed in getting a response.

When we were delivering all of those fliers, we were great at being responsive to the pager beeps (a.k.a. new leads coming in), and we sold a whole lot of homes way across town. "Way across town" is important. We were not averse to being inconvenienced. Driving farther than we wanted did not deter us. This evidenced our determination to succeed.

This story highlights a few things we did really right: We prospected with intensity and a great attitude. This resulted in meeting lots of people who found our passion enticing. When prospecting, we made sure to have compelling messages and calls-to-action. Compelling messages attract potential clients to your information, and the right call-to-action makes it non-confrontational and easy for them to reach out for that information. Finally, we followed up quickly and didn't give up. Our tenacity equated to business.

That first year we sold over eleven million in real estate.

Chuck says:

> Here is a pointer you need to take to heart. Commit to something, and don't ever give up. We weren't guaranteed results, but we were broke and knew we just had to work and work and work nonstop. It's truly a mindset. Life is hard, no matter what you do. You've probably heard that it has been said that dreams and aspirations without taking action are just wishes. I can honestly tell you that where I am today,

in all aspects of my life—including being an owner, father and husband—I am happy and fulfilled.

However, each aspect required enormous effort along the way. I could have stayed where I was, but I'm so glad that I chose to put forth the effort. The more it has paid off, the more motivated I am to continue to push hard today. I know that the effort is totally worth it.

I can't comprehend a person who does not strive to have a better life, especially in this country. I'm not just talking about money. For example, let me talk about my relationship with my wife. We live in a society where people give up on everything they do just because they can. But the funny part is, they are not any happier. My relationship with my wife, in both of our opinions, couldn't be any more perfect. This requires work. I think that everybody believes that the word "work" is a negative word. My wife and I are always saying that the relationship we have is based on a choice by two people: me and her. If we want to keep this relationship, which we both do, it will require some sacrifices and work, but the payoff far outweighs the effort. Quitting or being less than we are today is not an option. That is a choice we have both made.

It is the same in business. People aren't willing to make the sacrifices and put in the work that it takes to achieve the level of success that will give them better things for life. They quit, thinking that's the easier thing. But it's not, because they're miserable or broke. It just doesn't make sense. This culture has poisoned minds with the idea that everyone is entitled to great things, with little effort and right away. If it doesn't happen, you quit, which leaves you in a miserable place. The "it's all about me" mindset is debilitating. People who think they are entitled rarely break through any obstacles, and you can't experience success without breakthroughs. You need to embrace the process.

———

1. *Are you ready to prospect and follow up in an intense way?*

2. *Are you willing to put yourself in uncomfortable positions so that you improve your skills?*

3. *Have you considered the length of time you will have to persevere in order to be successful?*

CHAPTER SEVEN

GOOD THINGS HAPPEN WHEN YOU WORK

There's something really incredible that happens when you work hard. Good things start to happen. We have coached thousands of agents over the years, and there are some truths that we see play out over and over. One of them will completely shock you.

You will never have someone come and knock on the door to your house hoping that a real estate agent lives inside so that they can buy or sell with them.

I know. I just blew your mind. But, apparently, this is what many agents think will happen. They sit at home, day after day, wondering why they're not making any money. Crazy as it seems, you actually have to get out there and work. When Chuck and I finally get through to an agent and they start getting out there doing the business-producing activities they are supposed to be doing, they report stories of success and victory.

There's something else that happens too. Hard work, in the correct areas of your business, also brings delightful surprises—things you don't expect to happen.

There was a time when Chuck and I were showing a home for rent. We worked a lot with renters when we first started in the business because that's how we built relationships. Around here, renters don't always get the best treatment from agents because there's not a very big paycheck associated with these transactions. However, we saw a lot more value in renters than the money. We saw people who may eventually buy and, since we treated them with amazing customer service, they told other people about us. Referral business is sweet!

Anyway, on this particular day, after the potential renters left the showing, a car drove up to the front of the house as we were locking up. Chuck asked them if they wanted to look inside. It turned out they weren't renters, but they were buyers. That wonderful couple bought and sold with us a couple of times. When you're out working, great things happen.

There was a time when we were showing buyers houses. One of the houses we showed them was tenant occupied. After we were done showing the house, Chuck was talking with the tenants and asked them where they were going to move. The sad part was that they had just found out that morning that the house was going up for sale. They didn't find out via a phone call or a letter but by watching the sign post get installed. They were so sad because they had lived in that house for quite some time and loved it.

Chuck continued the conversation by asking, "Have you considered buying this house?" They hadn't considered it at all. In fact, it never occurred to them that they could afford to buy a house. We put them in touch with a lender, and they were qualified. We helped them write an offer on the house they already lived in, and you have never seen people more ecstatic and proud to own a home. It was a really awesome experience. Isn't it sad that it never occurred to the listing agent to ask that same question?

Be Willing to Jump When Opportunities Strike

One day I was door knocking while pushing my 2-year-old son, David, in a stroller. That's right; I was door knocking with my kid in a stroller. I came to a cul-de-sac and David reached out his hand just in time to brush against a prickly pear cactus. It was the kind that had the super fine spines and itchy powder, so he immediately rubbed his hands together—and screamed. There was a kind neighbor out who brought us inside, and we spent the next thirty minutes picking out all the little spines from his hands.

Her house was two houses down from an FSBO. As I left that kind woman's house, the owner of the FSBO was out in front of the house. Most mommies would have brought their exhausted 2-year-old home for some much needed rest, but I made a beeline for the FSBO. He was a crotchety old man, but guess what? He was ready to list.

Lesson: Sometimes it's ok for your kid to brush his hand against a cactus. If he hadn't done that, I would have been long gone down the street when that FSBO came over to check on his vacant house. Way to take one for the team, David!

Chuck and I took that listing. It was a two-story home at the end of a cul-de-sac, which would have been perfect except it backed to a canal with *huge* power lines. The house was vacant and we sat that house open all the time! (Chuck and Angela's definition of "all the time:" at least four days a week from nine or ten in the morning until it got dark. Yes, really, until it got dark. Not only did we sit open houses all the time but, quite often, so did our whole team. We learned early in our career that if we were going to be team leaders, we had to lead by doing and motivating.)

Those power lines were crazy huge. When you stood in the back yard, you could actually hear a buzzing sound. Chuck used to walk around the house with a silver bowl on his head—even in front of potential clients. There was a day when two ladies were in the backyard, and Chuck and I went out to talk with them. They were silent, with perplexed looks on their faces. One of them asked, "Can you hear that? What is that sound?"

Chuck answered in no uncertain terms, "What, that loud buzzing sound? It's coming from those enormous electrical lines, and all you have to do is wear this metal bowl on your head when you go outside!" I almost fell over. Chuck has a very uncanny way of joking around and winning clients over. Sometimes I can't believe what comes out of his mouth. He is the epitome of being as real as it gets.

We sold that home ourselves to someone who came into the open house unrepresented. We also picked up many buyers, some of which also had homes to sell.

Lesson: Take that listing with the enormous electrical lines in the back. You can sell it!

There are literally dozens of great stories I could tell you where wonderful things happen when you're out there working hard. Get that in your mind, and let it encourage you to push yourself hard! You absolutely need to embrace the process.

—

1. *Are you excited to get out there and work?*

2. *Can you see yourself experiencing the fun surprises that working hard can bring?*

3. *Are you willing to jump when opportunities strike?*

CHAPTER EIGHT

START WORKING ON YOUR MINDSET AND NEVER STOP

One of the most important things you need to do to live a high-performance life is to consistently work on your mindset. Neither Chuck nor I made it a priority to work on our mindset when we were new in the business. I am quite sure that if we had made it a priority from day one, our rough road would have been much smoother. Everyone who desires success must make working on your mindset a priority starting now, and never stopping. For many years at our brokerage, Chuck and I have been presenting to our agents every Monday morning. We call it Monday Morning Mindset, and it has literally changed our lives and the lives of many of our agents.

There are endless resources to strengthen your mind in a positive way: books, podcasts, videos, seminars and more. We'll get you started with some basics, and then you must implement mindset training into your regular schedule.

Mastering the Art of Being a Duck

People-pleasing is exhausting! Exhausting and disappointing. You can't please people all the time. In fact, you really can't please people most of the time. Focusing your time and energy on trying to make other people happy all the time will leave you emotionally bankrupt and worn out.

In sales, we work with a lot of people. To be great, you have to be able to communicate and appeal to a wide variety of personalities. Real estate is a customer service industry. At many levels, we are in the business of navigating through the stress of most people's largest purchase or sale, with skill and finesse, hoping to come out the other side with satisfied, happy clients.

There is a huge difference between striving to be the best professional and skilled REALTOR® possible and striving to please everyone along the way. The latter is impossible.

Great real estate agents—I mean, *really* great agents—will master the fine art of being a duck. Ducks have a preen gland at the base of their feathers. This gland causes oil to spread over their outer feathers; that's what makes the water roll off their backs. You can throw as much water at a duck as you want, but the water will not soak into its feathers.

REALTORS® need to be ducks.

The truth of the matter is, you can work heartily unto the Lord and have excellent process and procedure, along with stellar communication and negotiating skills, and people will still get mad. You cannot possibly be great and make everyone happy. Sometimes, being a duck is super helpful.

This is certainly not to say that great agents don't care about people. Not at all! Simply put, if someone doesn't like an agent's work or wants to complain about something, but the agent knows they have done their highest and best quality work, those complaints just roll right off that agent's back. In that circumstance, they are a duck.

Another aspect of mastering this fine art concerns prospecting. As we said before, prospecting is the activity of seeking out people who are looking to buy or sell and are willing to allow you to help them. In order to find these people, real estate agents have to talk to a whole lot of people who aren't looking to buy or sell or won't allow you to help them. Agents hear "no" a lot. It's inevitable, because you cannot find the yes's without many, many no's. One of Chuck's favorite lines is, "I'm looking for people who are looking for me."

The #1 Reason Most Agents Fail

Agents fail because they refuse to prospect or don't prospect nearly enough. It's an epidemic in this industry. We train both new and experienced agents, and just recently, during one class, I posed a couple of questions. The first question was:

On a scale of 1-10, with 10 being the greatest, how dedicated are you to succeeding in this business?

Out of a room of about thirty agents, all but two indicated they were a 10, and the other two said 9. This class was one in a series where agents were focusing on obtaining more listings. The next thing I asked them was:

How many of you got a listing or put a property under contract last week?

Most of them had not. The next thing I asked for was the most aggressive prospecting schedule in the room. In other words, I wanted to hear about the most robust prospecting week any of them had. This was the *most* productive schedule:

- Five hours of open house
- Two hours of door knocking
- A couple of hours on the phone responding to leads

What? No one else could touch that pathetic schedule. In fact, I know that most of the rest of the agents must not have prospected at all because most did not dare to even tell me their schedule.

A dedication of 10 does not equal less than ten hours of prospecting a week. I'd give that about a 4 on the dedication scale . . . maybe.

What holds agents back? One of the reasons is they have not mastered the art of being a duck. They let rejection and no's soak in.

Mastering the art of being a duck also involves how an agent responds to the lows of real estate. How do you react when a client you've been working with buys a new build without you? When you're trying hard to get your business off the ground or make it more lucrative and it's just not coming together, how do you respond? Right at the eleventh hour, the transaction you've poured hours into falls apart. What is your reaction? The answers will show where you are in the whole duck process.

When you find yourself in a bad situation and you persevere, letting all the bad roll off, there's a growth that happens. All successful agents have faced the lows of real estate and have grown from those experiences. Each time you demonstrate this type of resilience, you can grow in confidence, and it helps you face future lows in an even more masterful way.

The Turning Point that Could Have Been Our Breaking Point

Chuck and I were really broke when we first started in the business. "Really broke" isn't even a strong enough phrase. Is there something lower than flat broke? That was us. In our first six months working together, we did the best we could to work really hard. Looking back, we didn't know what we were doing at all, but we were giving it all we had. About six months into our partnership—in December of 2001—we had five deals scheduled to close. We had felt we were about to turn the corner.

All five of these deals were entrusted to a certain lender that had talked us into using her. As I explained before, Chuck and I are a bit on the extreme side, and "diversification of lenders" wasn't yet in our vocabulary. All five of those deals fell out that month. All of them. Every single one.

All of them.

If I tell you it was devastating, that's not a dramatization. We were already flat broke and even with those closings, we would have been just on the other side of broke. One December night, after the fall-out, we were sitting in my backyard. With my head in my hands, I asked Chuck, "Do you think your mom and dad will let us move in?" This was a huge low—one of the worst in our entire career.

Something caught fire in us after that. We could have both gotten jobs . . . yuck! It was the perfect set of circumstances to quit. Chuck and I had children to care for and responsibilities to fulfill. However, praise God, we both had the seed of this wonderful fruit that comes from mastering the art of being ducks. A fire had been lit. Our desire to succeed far outweighed any hesitations we may have been harboring, and certain things started to happen.

Chuck knew a guy who knew a guy, and Chuck got us an awesome listing.

Actually, the truth is, it wasn't that easy at all. The listing has a history. Chuck had known an investor and a builder a couple of years before having the opportunity to list this property. In fact, he had introduced the investor to the builder. The investor ended up partnering with the builder and built two custom homes. Unfortunate circumstances prevented Chuck from getting those listings at first. Another real estate agent actually got the listings. However, there was a turn of events.

Our Long Shot (a.k.a. You've Gotta Ask Before You Can Receive)

The good news is that the other real estate agent couldn't sell the homes. I don't know if the Lord specifically orchestrated this fortunate turn of events or if He just allowed it to happen. Either way, two years later, the investor decided to give us a shot at one of the listings, a little baby shot . . . a teeny weeny baby shot. I think he gave us three months to sell it and prove ourselves. Keep in mind, the market time for a custom home back then well exceeded three months.

The home was in the Sanctuary, a gated neighborhood in Ahwatukee, and was vacant, so we sat it open all the time.

Just a reminder: Chuck and Angela's definition of "all the time" is at least four days a week from nine or ten in the morning until it got dark. Yes, really, until it got dark.

One day at the open house *the guy* came in. I call him *the guy* because he really was. Actually, I should call him *the man*! Here's the story.

The man's name is Mark. He came into the open house one day, walked around for about twenty minutes, and then left. Mark was not very open to conversation, and we had no clue at the time how to engage clients in open houses. Later that same day, Mark came back with his family and spent a good thirty to forty-five minutes in the home. None of the family would engage with us at all before hightailing it out of there.

Chuck and I held hands and began to cry and feel sorry for ourselves. Why didn't they like us? Why did they ignore us? Maybe we're just not good agents.

Okay, *stop*! That didn't happen at all.

Chuck is a duck. We had three months to sell that listing, and that guy was interested. Chuck was further fueled by the challenge of proving to the investor that we could sell that house. Remember, Chuck is extremely competitive. He lets nothing stand in his way.

Less than two minutes after they walked out, Chuck bolted out the front door. Wondering what the heck he was doing, I watched him through the window. As Mark and his family were pulling away, Chuck ran down the driveway and jumped in front of Mark's truck, putting both of his hands on the hood. Mark rolled down his window, kind of confused, nervous and laughing all at the same time. Mr. Brash New Yorker asked, "Why ain't you buying this house?"

Mark replied, "I don't understand what you're talking about."

"You came in twice today, once earlier by yourself. You spent about half an hour here, clearly showing interest in the home. Then you come back with your wife and kids, spent about another half an hour in the home, never asking even one question, and then you leave. To me, common sense would say that you're clearly interested in the home."

As Mark laughed in amusement, he said, "Yes, you're right. We do love the house, but we can't afford it."

"How do you know, if you haven't even tried to make an offer?" Chuck pressed.

"Listen, not only do I think I can't afford it, but I also have a house to sell."

With conviction in his voice, Chuck replied, "Why don't we take a look at your home and see what we can get for it and then put in an offer on this one contingent upon the sale of your house. You've got nothing to lose."

That's when Mark wrote down his contact information and said, "Give me call. Take a look at my home, and we'll talk about it."

Really? Is that the sales tactic that works? The big New Yorker runs down the driveway toward the SUV like the Incredible Hulk? Jumps in front of this poor guy with his wife and kids inside like he's about to deliver a Hulk Smash and basically roars, "What's a matta for you?" Why yes, it is!

If you don't ask for business, you won't get it. As aggressive as Chuck seemed through this example, he was entirely sincere. It wasn't a sales pitch. Chuck perceived Mark's want and simply assertively pushed him down the path of discovery in order to help him get what he ultimately wanted. This was one of our biggest aha moments. One of the secrets of sales that we empower our agents with is this one profound line: If you don't ask, you can't receive.

Twenty-three days into us having that listing, we helped Mark write an offer—an offer that was contingent upon the sale of his home, which was not even on the market yet. Miraculously, the offer was accepted, and we were under contract. We now had just a little more than two months to list and put Mark's house under contract. His house was a high-ticket home too, plus Mark needed almost top of the market price to make everything work.

Sixty-four days later, Mark's house went under contract. It was literally *days* before the contingency timeframe would expire. I wish I could explain how hard we worked to get that house sold. The determination we had was unshakeable. Don't get me wrong, we were increasingly anxious and nervous as the days wore on. However, we're ducks! All the negative thoughts of possible failure rolled off our backs. It didn't paralyze us but drove us to flier more, door knock more and sit that house open more. It was worth it!

This fantastic listing steam rolled into an unbelievable line of business. We listed and sold the investor's other home next door, sold a Forte spec home in the same neighborhood, an FSBO home across the street and eventually met *the family*. That story comes later. Please know that when we were laser focused on getting Mark's home sold, it wasn't in anticipation of this other business. We weren't even thinking about possible future business. We were simply working at our utmost excellence to get the deal done.

When you're out there working intensely, other things happen. All that other business didn't happen by accident. Neighbors were watching the number of open houses we conducted and the number of times we delivered fliers while out door knocking. We were focused on serving our client, and that got noticed. Don't underestimate who is watching your actions—both good and bad—while you conduct your business.

There's something else that we didn't tell you about Mark. We didn't know it ourselves until later on. Before he owned the house, Mark would drive by fairly often, when the first agent had the listing, just to look at the front of it. He would never call the number on the sign. He didn't think he could afford it and didn't want to talk with an agent. He told us that he kept waiting for an open house (which he never found). The moral to this part of the story is two-fold: First, don't let *anyone* tell you open houses don't work! Second, don't be a weenie when it comes to open houses. Remember our definition of sitting a house open all the time.

Oh, by the way, in the years that followed, my sweet husband would get a phone call every once in a while from Mark. Mark would be walking around his home, enjoying and treasuring the fact that he owned it, and he would say to my husband, "I can't believe I own this home! Thank you for stopping my car."

Lesson: Grow whatever glands you need to grow in order to become a duck. It's worth the effort.

Kick Some Grass Over that Poop

We have had many dogs over the years and currently have two: a Bulldog named Bubbles and Buddy, a Goldendoodle.

We are so busy with work and kids that the dogs don't get walked much. When we do take the opportunity to walk them, it's a predictably hilarious ritual. One of the things Bubbles always does on walks is poop. *Always*. She's amazing. She can always conjure up a poop. And she has an awesome ritual when she poops. Many of you who have dogs will recognize it; not all dogs have this ritual but enough for it to be something many know. First, there's the poop, stinky and yucky. Then there's the dance where grass is flying backwards, covering up that poop. Then there's the burst of energy in the form of a run in the opposite direction of that poop.

I think Bubbles is on to something.

Life gives us a whole lot of poops. In real estate, we deal with so many people that the poops are everywhere. Chuck and I often explain to our agents that we are dealing with most people's largest financial transaction of their lives, and the act of moving itself is one of the highest-stress activities that people can do. Under these circumstances, the best side of people is not what we're normally dealing with. Quite often, it's the worst.

When you strip down a real estate transaction, it's actually just a process. A process is simply a series of factual events that happen in a certain order. The emotions we attach to this process are what make it stressful. With high emotions come all kinds of irrational behaviors. The great agents don't get themselves emotionally involved in the transaction. They don't get insulted by low-ball offers or offended by a long repair list. In fact, spectacular agents are able to diffuse the highly-emotional moments and navigate through the overreactions and offense.

In essence, they kick grass onto that poop.

One of the greatest qualities an agent can have is to be able to disconnect from the high emotions associated with so much of real estate. When prospecting, for example, if you run into someone who's acting like a poop, agents have a choice how they will react.

1. They allow themselves to be so affected by the negative experience that they actually start smelling bad too. Then, even though they try to keep going, they already stink, so their subsequent attempts also offend. The result is little or no success.

2. Great agents figuratively cover that poop with fresh green grass. They embrace the experience as part of the process and walk away unscathed, ready to try again. Their subsequent attempts aren't tainted, and success is surely right around the corner!

Mindset is powerful, and you have control over yours. The effort you put into your outlook and reactions, your thoughts and perceptions, matters; a positive mindset will be greatly rewarded.

Maybe, next time you're door knocking, grab a handful of sweet, fresh grass and put it in your pocket just in case you need to throw some over your shoulder as you walk away from a poop.

An Agent's Terminal Disease

Are you full of disease? No, I'm not talking about a physical sickness but rather a mindset disease. Chuck and I have studied agents—literally thousands of them—and we are now experts at detecting certain kinds of mindset diseases. One of the most terminal of all the mindset diseases is the victim mentality.

- Victim mentality, like all diseases, has symptoms. Some of the most common symptoms are:

- Deficiency of personal responsibility—Characterized by the inability to take any personal responsibility when things go wrong or aren't working.

- Chronic blaming—Due to the first symptom causing the delusion that nothing is ever their fault, they point their fingers at someone or something else as the cause of the problem.

- Fever of rationalization—Burning up with self-pity, this person can quickly and creatively drum up stories and circumstantial evidence proving their innocence in a situation.

- Cycle of self-pity—Victims inherently feel sorry for themselves, which cycles into the rationalization, which exacerbates the self-pity.

- Blurry vision—This disease affects the vision of the patient, causing them to only be able to focus on the problem, not the solution. This impairment often causes whining and complaining.

- Attention deficit—Feeling sorry for themselves, victim patients want attention. While whining and crying from their blurry vision, they are seeking to attract attention from others as a form of validation for their behavior.

There are many other lesser symptoms, but if you recognize one or more of these in your life, you need a prescription—STAT! How can you get on the road to recovery? There are several forms of treatment; depending upon the depth of your disease, it may take either a few small adjustments or months of rehabilitation. Nevertheless, the victim mentality, if caught and treated, is curable.

Treatment steps:

1. First, the patient must acknowledge the victim behavior. Oftentimes, the symptoms are obvious to everyone but the patient. A suggestion is to journal for a couple of weeks. Every time a "victim" thought or action occurs, write it down. Another method is to ask the people closest to you, whom you trust to speak the brutal truth, to tell you when you are acting like a victim.

2. Next, change those thoughts intentionally into positive, internally-focused expressions. "Internally-focused" refers to your locus of control. People with an external locus of control are victims and have the symptoms listed above. People with an internal locus of control believe they have some sort of control or responsibility in every situation. These people are empowered because they see themselves as having an effect on their own life and circumstances to some degree rather than being someone stuff just happens to.

   Positive expression doesn't necessarily mean rainbows and unicorns. For example, if a victim thought is, "I can't believe that guy ran the red light and plowed into me," the positive thought might be, "I had part responsibility in the accident. I could have glanced left and right before proceeding, and perhaps I could have avoided the accident." Another example is, instead of thinking, "All the people who ever come into my open houses are either looky loos or have an agent already," you may say, "I'm not as effective in open houses as I want to be, so I'm going to seek out training to have better scripts and techniques for overcoming objections."

3. Then, internalize those new, empowering thought patterns and take action on them. Be that agent who strives to improve yourself because you attribute your lack of success to something you can change or control. When you're feeling sorry for yourself, set a timer and give yourself two full minutes to have your pity party. When that alarm sounds, move on with confidence to the next productive activity. Decide that you can choose your attitude.

4. Be thankful! Gratitude is the best antidote to the poison of the victim disease. When you clear your blurry vision

by focusing on all of the things you are grateful for (and you have a lot), everything seems brighter and better. Opportunities pop up all around you. Plus, you're a whole lot more fun to be around.

A Suggestion to Help Radically Improve Your Mindset (and Your Results)

Chuck and I want to make a suggestion to you that can radically change your mindset. Most people will decide if they are a victim or if they're not. They will decide if other people are victims or if they aren't.

That's too black and white.

The truth is, we are all victims in at least one way and perhaps in many ways. Being a victim can be compartmentalized or situational. Someone can take full responsibility for their actions in one area of their life but act like a total victim in another.

How can this be?

We are all works in progress. There are so many facets to life—financial, professional, spiritual, interpersonal, physical, social, and the list goes on. Furthermore, any one category of our life has strengths and weaknesses. In the area of your career, for example, you can be victorious in some aspects and working failures in others.

Chuck and I constantly challenge each other in the area of victim mentality. It's so off-putting to us that we are passionate about facing our own victim tendencies. We have mutually agreed to hold each other accountable in this area. We are committed to owning our behaviors, attitudes, thought processes and reactions. Why are we so confrontational with each other in this area? It's because we love each other. We want the best for each other and, as business owners and leaders, we can't afford to fall into a lazy-minded, victim mentality.

You should not tolerate it from yourself either.

Our suggestion to you would be to find yourself someone to keep you accountable. Could be a fellow agent, your spouse, a parent, a friend . . . anyone you can trust to hold your feet to the fire and keep you accountable to yourself and your positive mindset.

Chuck says:

> We could have been victims many times through-out our career, but we would not be where we are if we had not resisted this mentality. We could have blamed our first brokerage for our failure. We could have blamed our franchise for our difficulties. We could have used the excuse of being new to the area or inexperienced in business. The list could go on and on. Anyone can sit and think about someone or something to blame.
>
> One of the biggest ways you can grow as a person and successful professional is to recognize—and squash—the victim mindset when it creeps in. This can be very hard to do because it forces you to rid yourself of your pride and ego and become humble and accountable. Remember, you are in control of how you react to a circumstance.

———

1. *Are you convinced that working on your mindset is crucial?*

2. *Have you noticed any victim mentality in your own life?*

3. *Can you picture yourself facing frustration with a great attitude?*

CHAPTER NINE

PUT THE RIGHT PEOPLE IN YOUR SUCCESS CORNER

"You're the average of the five people you
spend the most time with.""

—JIM ROHN

Who you surround yourself with is so important. If you can wrap your mind around this concept and really embrace it, your life will change. God created us to be in community with others and, by nature, we affect each other. Those effects can be both positive and negative. On a regular basis, you need to make an analysis of those closest to you. Do you have people surrounding you that are heading in the same direction you want to go? You need people who are bigger thinkers than you, more successful than you, know more than you and have the character qualities you want to develop. Basically, surround yourself with what you want your future self to be like in one or more ways.

Conversely, you may need to cut out relationships that weigh you down. We are not saying to go home and say to your spouse, "Chuck and Angela told me I need to cut you out of my life." And no, you may not kick out your kids. However, in all seriousness, if you're working hard to build success in your real estate career and you have naysayers surrounding you, cut them out! It's hard enough to build your business without allowing negative people to discourage you. For the most part, you are in control of who you are around. Choose carefully.

Don't Let Vampires Suck You Dry

People are obsessed with vampires. Even our youngest son, Bentley, is obsessed at the moment. In fact, he is afraid of bats that apparently live in our garage because when they bite you, you become a "vohmpire" (that's how he says it, and, oh, by the way, "vohmpires" eat "hangabers," according to Bentley).

I don't know about the reality of immortal, blood-sucking, never-aging, love-the-dark vampires, but I do whole-heartedly believe in the most dangerous of vampires.

The kind of vampires I'm thinking of are the most lethal of all in the history of vampires. They roam the earth, and the naked eye cannot necessarily identify them. They look like the rest of us and can even walk around in broad daylight without scorching a bit.

They don't suck your blood. That's amateur to them. They take something much more valuable: they suck your *energy*.

Energy vampires are everywhere. Cunningly, they seem like normal humans at first as they engage with you. You may start a conversation with them and even become friends. Even worse, one may be placed in your family. Or, the worst yet, you may marry one.

No matter how deeply these vampires embed themselves into your life, they all want the same thing from you: your energy. They suck it right out of you. They are negative, discouraging, ho-hum creatures that, when they're done with you, leave you hardly able to breathe. You are left slumped over and spent with no motivation to do anything better than sit in front of the TV with a gallon of ice cream.

The most terrible thing about energy vampires is that if you allow yourself to be surrounded by one or more of them for too long, you become one too.

Energy vampires can be REALTORS® too. You have to watch out for them. Here's how you can identify one:

1. They love to gossip.

2. According to them, the market is always bad.

3. When they prospect (if they prospect), no one is ever looking to buy or sell.

4. They will complain about the cross-sale agent, their client, their office . . . well, they just complain.

5. They are never to blame nor are they the problem. It's always someone or something else.

6. Excuses are a part of their everyday life.

7. *Beware:* They may even act this way with smiles on their faces.

If you are a real estate agent, or looking to become one, be very, very careful of these dangerous vampires. They will hinder or even sabotage your business. If you see one, you should shout, "You can't have my energy!" and run away. That oughta stop 'em.

We have been in the presence of many energy vampires. There were a few times we got close to being brought down by one, as agents, team leaders and brokerage owners.

We had a client we'll call Steve, because that was his name. We helped him find a home. He was so negative and demanding that the whole transaction sucked us dry. But, we closed the deal and then swore to each other we'd never work with him again.

Years later, Steve called us up. He needed us to sell his home. I'm not kidding when I say that we actually said to each other, "Was he really that bad? Nah! Probably not." It was a decent sales price, and the market was pretty good. We took the listing.

Chuck is great with clients. People love him. Don't get me wrong, he can get worked up, but he's great under pressure and gets sharper as the intensity goes up.

Chuck wanted to punch Steve in the face. It was *that* bad. (He didn't, by the way.) Hindsight is 20/20, but I can see now that Steve was a vampire, and Chuck suffered energy drain every time he was with Steve. It wasn't worth the money.

Lesson: If you hated working with someone the first time, you'll probably hate it again. It's really not worth your time, regardless of the money. Important side note: There's a difference in having your energy taken for no good reason (money is not always a good reason) and allowing a vampire in for a while for the purpose of serving someone in need. When you're serving a vampire, they can't make you become one of them, no matter how hard they try.

There was another time, very early in our brokerage years, when we met another businesswoman. We had several occasions to work with her and got to know her pretty well. As I've mentioned before, starting up our brokerage was really hard in every way—physically, emotionally, financially—and there were times where we couldn't see the point of it all.

Anyway, the woman was a vampire, but we didn't recognize it in our weakened state. We had forgotten that the Lord had led us to opening the brokerage and that the purpose was to serve Him through serving agents. The vampiress brought us down the path that highlighted that we were making a whole bunch of money before as agents and not so much as brokerage owners. She talked with us about how much better it might be to ditch the brokerage and just worry about ourselves. She highlighted all the negative things and sucked almost all of the rest of our energy out. We were two or three vampiress sips away from becoming one too.

Obviously, it didn't happen, thank God. Our point is that everyone is susceptible to being sucked dry by one of these creatures. Don't forget to stay on guard and when you recognize one, you know what to do:

Yell, "You can't have my energy!" and run away.

Chuck says:

> There are some important things to take away from these negative people (so-called "energy vampires"). One, it is crucial, and I mean *crucial*, to surround yourself with like-minded, successful people. Take a look around your office. First and foremost, do you have an office at all? Does your company even offer the opportunity to be around success? If you have an office, what is it like? Are agents feeding off of one another positively, or are they gossiping and complaining about everything? Who are the top producers in your office? What kind of production do they do? Are they around? One of our biggest attributes as a company is the culture of professional,

successful agents. We intentionally surround like-minded, driven people around each other in an incredible office. We believe God created us as a body. So, we don't feed into the crap most companies sell about not needing a good physical space. As owners of a company, that is a big lie they sell so that they save money!

Rainbows, Rocket Ships, Cheerleaders and Mother Theresa

The people you surround yourself with are crucial to your personal growth and success. You can only bring yourself so far. We were created to be in community with other people, and that community will shape and mold you. If this is true, and it is, you should be very concerned about whom you allow to shape and mold you. We've already discussed an example of people you shouldn't surround yourself with—those energy-sucking types— but with whom should you surround yourself?

This is a question that you should be constantly asking yourself. The answer, over the span of your life, may have some consistency. For example, we should all surround ourselves with people who make us feel happy and with whom we can laugh. Laughter is one of the tools God gave Chuck and me that has blessed us abundantly. We laugh easily and often! I never want to lose the influence of laughter in my life. In fact, the agents and team members who tend to stick around the longest have this quality as well.

There are many other qualities that may be a constant search for you. The name of this section is *Rainbows, Rocket Ships, Cheerleaders and Mother Theresa* because each of these represents qualities in people that we believe we constantly want as influences in our lives.

Rainbows

Rainbows are awe-inspiring. Every once in a while we'll have the most spectacular rainbows in Arizona. Not too long ago, our family witnessed a triple rainbow from our backyard. It's almost impossible to look at a 180-degree arc of a triple rainbow and not be wowed! We all took out our cell phones and cameras and took picture after picture and video after video. Our busy world stopped for several minutes, and we just stood in wonder. That day, we couldn't stop talking about it, and it lifted us up. We need people in our lives that have that effect on us, those that make us stop and observe and those that lift us up for the whole day, week or month. These people can help you to be inspired to do more, to dream more and to achieve more.

Rocket Ships

Rocket ships are powerful, focused and accurate. The power needed for a rocket ship depends upon where it's going. For example, if a rocket ship is going to escape the earth's atmosphere enough to get into orbit, it takes a certain speed and thrust to do so. Then, once in orbit, it has to maintain a certain speed to stay there. If that speed is not maintained, that rocket ship falls back down to the earth.

If a rocket ship is designed to completely escape the gravitational pull of the earth and the sun, it takes a series of multi-stage rockets, a whole lot more thrust plus a certain speed. In short, it's a lot more effort, and, depending upon how far into space it is going, the process is more difficult and demands more resources.

Finally, if that ship has a destination—for example, the moon—then there is a demand for focus and accuracy. Without focus and accuracy, all that power, speed and resources will have been wasted since the target was completely missed. We want people in our lives that demonstrate these qualities.

In business, the thrust, speed and power of the rocket ship is a great analogy for the effort and intensity needed to do something great! Furthermore, there can't just be a one-time thrust. Business growth demands a series of intense bursts to break through barriers. In fact, barriers will always come. By having people in your life that have broken through and continue to break through, you can be encouraged, mentored, inspired, pushed and challenged.

The focus and accuracy of these people help to hone all of the efforts into a destination. People around us who have written goals and plans teach us to utilize our resources in a way that gains the results we're looking for. These people can reel us in if we have gone off track. They can push us harder in the right direction because they know how to do this themselves.

Cheerleaders

The role of cheerleaders is self-explanatory. Real estate is hard. You need people around you who tell you that you can do it! They are constantly singing, "Two, four, six eight, who do we appreciate? *You, you, you!*" When you feel like giving up, they don't let you. My husband is my biggest cheerleader, and I am his.

We are our agents' biggest cheerleaders. We laugh when people say to us, "We don't want to be just a number at your office." Currently, we have almost 700 agents. I know almost all of their names. The truth is, you will be more of a number at some offices of only twenty agents than at ours. It's not about the number of agents. It's about the culture, leadership and relationship. We not only cheer our agents on but give them tangible tools, systems, training and guidance that support their growth. Find your cheerleaders, both personally and professionally. It will positively affect your business!

Mother Theresa

Finally, Mother Theresa represents a deep, genuine care that surpasses circumstances and time. We all need those invaluable people that surround us with as close to an unconditional caring for us and our businesses as is possible. People who truly care fuel passion, and you cannot be successful without passion.

Throughout your career, and life in general, you may find that the qualities you need reinforced and strengthened will change. Just as often as you intentionally set goals, you should evaluate the people who surround you. Are there those who need to have less influence? Do you need to seek out some different relationships? Are there strong and steady people you need to thank for their relationship? Be intentional.

———

1. *Do you have people in your life who will encourage you?*

2. *Are there some people you know you need to back away from?*

3. *Will you seek out resources to feed your mind positive things?*

CHAPTER TEN

WORK WITH INTENTION, INTENSITY AND FOCUS

I t's so easy to let days, weeks, months or even years go by without really engaging in life. Social media, TV, and a host of other distractions can draw you down a path of living a numb life. We have to constantly refocus ourselves and make conscious decisions to live with intention, intensity and focus. A successful real estate career demands these things. The great news is you can strengthen and develop yourself and create habits in all three of these areas.

Kids at a Lemonade Stand: A Lesson in Intention

I recently Googled "lemonade stand" and found 5,600,000 entries. You can find articles showing step by step, detail after detail, how to run an amazing lemonade stand. I even found out that the first recorded lemonade stand was operated in 1873 by a 10-year-old boy named Edward Bok. He records in his 1922 autobiography, *The Americanization of Edward Bok,* the story of how he used to sell ice water for a penny on the hot streets of Brooklyn. Apparently, he had a lot of competition, so one day he squeezed a little lemon into the water and—TADA—lemonade. Bottom line: there's a lot of information about lemonade stands.

In our neighborhood, we see lemonade stands quite frequently. I didn't take a survey of all the kids, but I can safely guess that they didn't pore over the 5,600,000 entries in preparation for their business. In fact, I'll bet they didn't even look at one. Those hopeful kids gathered what they needed, made the lemonade, and dreamed of the fortune they would have by the end of the day.

The kids shout out to passersby, encouraging them to stop and grab a cold one. Unfortunately, the people passing by are often jogging, riding a bike, walking their dogs, rollerblading or driving by at 35 miles per hour. I don't know about you, but when I go out to ride my own version of the Tour de France, I'm not carrying any quarters. Those kids' only hope are attracting people who plan ahead to buy lemonade, getting their parents to come and buy a glass or counting on drivers of the cars speeding by to have nothing better to do than to stop for a glass of something they probably won't enjoy.

Just the other day, as we were driving 35 miles per hour past a lemonade stand, the girl shouted out in frustration, "Why don't you stop?" and actually stomped her feet. I'd like to tell you that the little girl's frustration melted my heart, that her attempt at entrepreneurship moved us to pull over for the two minutes it would have taken to reward her efforts. We didn't.

You know, most real estate agents aren't that much different than that little girl. They decide to do an open house and, even though there's a wealth of knowledge and training about how to conduct a great one, they don't take the time or make the effort to study. In fact, I just Googled "open house," and the entries far outnumbered that of "lemonade stand." In fact, there were 349,000,000 entries.

These hopeful agents set out a few open house signs and sit on the couch, waiting for people to come in. If people do come in, the agent may or may not engage in good conversation. After two and a half hours, the agent decides to close up early, stomps their feet and shouts, "Open houses don't work!"

Chuck and I have been in real estate longer than some and not as long as others. However, we have a perspective that few have. As agents, we ranked in the top one percent in the nation for several years in a row. As team leaders, we ran one of the top teams in the nation. Currently, our brokerage has been number one in production in the East Valley of the Phoenix Metropolitan area for seven years in a row. The Lord has caused us to experience success from these many perspectives and we believe, with all our hearts, that we can help agents succeed. Our book was conceived from our desire to speak the truth to the agents who are serious about succeeding.

What if you were really intentional with your business?

Kids at a Lemonade Stand: The Success Remix

Let's say a kid was really serious about having a successful lemonade stand. What needs to be considered?

- The quality of the lemonade: Is it delicious? Will it be cold?

- Supply: Will they have enough?

- Timing: When and for how long will the stand be open?

- Staff: Who will help, and what's the split of profits?

- Compelling message: What will you tell people about the reason why they should buy?

- Location: Where can the stand be located to maximize appropriate exposure?

Let's focus on the location for a moment. At first thought, putting your lemonade stand on a busy street could make sense. However, although many people may see you on a busy street, they may not take the time to stop. If you move your lemonade stand to a quieter neighborhood street, people may be more willing to stop, but the exposure is limited. You could knock on all the neighbor's doors and announce your lemonade stand, which could increase traffic. But the best location would probably be near a park with a sporting event or tennis courts where lots of people could be playing and getting thirsty.

Let's say the location at that park is golden—lots of people and moms with purses. What if you also had a compelling message? What if you had a large sign that announced, "Ice-cold lemonade—50 cents. Help me save for a new bike!" Possibly some people would decide that it's a worthy cause and buy lemonade they don't even want. Heck, they may even pay a buck for it. There is merit to thinking things through and being prepared.

What to Consider Before Hosting an Open House

Now, let's say we have a great agent—one who is serious about their business and understands the importance of prospecting. This agent wants to do an open house. What needs to be considered?

- The quality of the home: Is it a home with curb appeal? Is the home appealing in the agent's market? Are there detriments to the home?

- Preparation: Did the agent preview in the neighborhood? Did the agent door knock to invite to the open house? Did the agent announce this open house to their center of influence?

- Timing: When and for how long will the house be open?

- Staff: Who will help, and what's the split of commission?

- Compelling message: What will you tell people about the reason why they should buy or sell with you? A personal brochure is an excellent way to display things about yourself that may appeal to potential clients. The contents of this brochure can highlight what is interesting and unique about who you are personally. Hobbies or unique places you have visited could spark conversations, which can lead to building rapport. You can also include a few testimonials.

- Location: Where can the open house be held to maximize appropriate exposure?

These aren't all the considerations, but the point is, there are considerations. Don't get us wrong: preparing to prepare to prepare is the death of a real estate agent. However, a REALTOR® who wants huge success needs to work thoughtfully through their business.

Chuck says:

> While we are on the topic of open houses, first let's just say that doing open houses is not just about plopping a bunch of open house signs around. There are definitely some strategies to maximize your time

while sitting a home open. The location is important choose a home in an area where you want to work. Keep in mind, if a prospect walks through a home and doesn't like that home, they're in that area for a reason. That's where they're looking to buy. So, if you're sitting a home across town, do you really want to be driving across town to show potential buyers that you picked up at that open house?

I will never forget the time that Angela and I were sitting a house open in El Mirage, which we never even knew existed. It was one of the first listings we got. Just to give you an idea, it was about a 50-60 minute drive for us. As buyers were coming in to check out the house, I kept saying to Angela, "Don't make eye contact with anyone because the last thing we want is to pick up buyers out here." Boy, did that make for an interesting open house.

Next, consider price range. Pick a price range that you are looking to work in. For example, if you want to break into the luxury market, sit a higher-priced home open. That is how Angela and I broke into that market.

One of the first luxury open houses we sat was priced at $1,100,000 and sat in a gated community called Sanctuary. This particular home was a very important turning point in our career. It was a custom spec home built by Forte. The house was new, and one of the owners of Forte homes, John Corcoran, had his wife, Sharon, sit the home open normally. They just didn't trust any other agents to represent the home well enough to prospects. Sharon was about to have a baby, and we asked permission to sit that home open in her absence. Thankfully, they agreed. Little did John and Sharon know that this generous gesture blessed us abundantly, and they had a great impact in our growing success.

We sat that house open almost every day, all day. Not only did we eventually sell that home, but it led to a lot of other amazing business. In fact, Forte homes was developing another community where we sold many of the lots and build-to-suit homes.

I'll never forget sitting in there as two broke agents saying, "Oh my gosh! This house is so unbelievable! Can you imagine living in this? What kind of people can afford to live here?" It was actually like sitting in a house that should be on *Lifestyles of the Rich and Famous;* at least, it seemed that way to us at the time. Luxury homes can be like a buyer magnet at times. Everybody wanted to stop by and see that beautiful home. We would start a conversation with people who came in, and they would ask, "How much is this home?" We would tell them, waiting for the, "Oh my gosh, I can't believe it's that much!" comment. They would say, "Oh, that's a little out of our price range. We're only looking to spend $800,000." Barely containing our excitement, we would think to ourselves, "Twist my arm! I guess we'll work with you." Actually, we would say, "But of course we can help you find a home." What started happening was we were picking up these buyers in higher price ranges.

Can you imagine how this felt for us, working with these clients? We began to receive paychecks ranging from fifteen to twenty-five thousand dollars! Angela and I were saying to each other, "Can this really be real, making this kind of money?" Remember, we went from being totally broke to having months where we would make sixty to seventy-five thousand dollars! To us, that was insane. This was not only career-changing but also life-changing.

We sat that million-dollar house open so much that the homeowners' association of that gated subdivision connected the "0" for "operator" on the guard gate keypad to Angela's cell phone so that the clients could gain access to the subdivision easier. No, I'm not kidding. That's the way we roll. What's actually hysterical is that years later, Angela's number was still connected to the operator button on this same gate. Everynow and then, her phone would ring at all hours of the night because someone hit that button to get into the gate. Angela got a kick out of that and would answer the phone all the time saying, "Sanctuary gate!" There would be all sorts of people calling, including pizza guys. Angela would badger them by saying, "Is the pizza hot? Is the pizza good? Are you wearing shoes?" just to bust their chops. Another time, there was a plumber that needed to get into a house. There she went again, badgering, "Are you going to do a good job? Are you going to fix the problem?" She loved being the Sanctuary gate keeper. I think they must have finally caught on because it stopped. She was fired!

Now, I'm not saying that just because you sit a higher-end home open that you're going to break into that market, but at least it gives you that potential opportunity to meet the people looking to buy in that price range. Believe me, potential clients will not come into the home, look at you and think, "Those don't look like agents who can sell in this price range."

Look for homes that don't have potential detriments to certain buyers. For example, take single-level homes. You may consider, if you're working in the Phoenix area, choosing a single-level home over a two-story because more people prefer a single-level to a two-story. Examples of potential detriments vary from area to area, but some example may be homes that back to busy streets or large power lines, or those that are close to train tracks or airports. Another detriment may be a home that has bad curb appeal. I'm not saying that you would never sit those homes open; however, given the choice, make a wise one. Remember, potential prospects are following signs to see the house that's open. If they drive up and see a detriment, they may just drive off, and you lose the opportunity to meet them. If the house doesn't meet their needs from the outside, they're not going to walk into the home just because they feel sorry for the agents and they want to give you an opportunity to pick them up as buyers.

Agents always ask me, "What days should I sit a house open? What times?" First, let's address the times. Most agents pick timeframes like 10-2 or 12-4. What's up with these four-hour timeframes? Who the heck came up with this concept? When we worked, we sat houses open from 8:30 in the morning to 6:30 at night. This is what we did for a living, and we worked that way. Are you a part-time agent or a full-time agent?

What about which days are better than others? Although weekends are generally going to attract more potential clients, what I say to agents is that if you're not doing an open house, what are you going to be doing? Are you going to be sitting in your own house instead of an open? Where are you going to have a better chance of meeting a buyer? When is the last time someone walked into your personal home looking to buy a house? Most agents just look for a way not to work. I'll challenge any lazy agent who says open houses don't work. What better way is there for any agent to get in front of a buyer or seller (yes, I said seller) for FREE than an open house? There are no good excuses for an agent not to sit open houses. Now, I understand you could be at a company that doesn't have a lot of listings, or maybe you are a new agent and having a hard time finding listings. That is one of the reasons you want to align yourself with a good company that has a lot of listings.

I Want To Be a Boy Scout: A Lesson in Intensity

We have six children. We call them *his*, *mine*, *ours* and *theirs*. Chuck has two children from his first marriage. I have one from mine. We have one together, and we have two that we adopted. It's a blessed combination, and each of them is unique and amazing in their own way. If you are a parent, you will agree that children will teach parents all kinds of lessons. Children are the source of delight, awe, joy, and great big headaches.

Let's talk about *ours*. His name is Matthew, and he is definitely delightful (much like his mother). Matthew has a quick wit, and his humor is super sophisticated (which he gets from Chuck). Here is the first of a couple of quotes from Matthew Fazio:

"I want to be a Boy Scout so I can earn badges, punch bears in the face and ride a donkey."

Note to the readers: Matthew has no intention of being a Boy Scout.

Another quote demands some background. We take our kids to a summer camp in Prescott, Arizona, each year. It's a Christian Bible camp called Camp Saguaro Cedarbrook. (As a side note, it's absolutely an amazing and affordable camp that our kids LOVE and wouldn't miss for anything. If you live in the area, you should check it out for your kids. You can find more info at www.SaguaroCampCedarbrook.com.)

As we are almost at the camp, we pass a property that has large bronze statues of different dinosaurs and other creatures. The anticipation of seeing these bronzes is part of the tradition of summer camp. One of the dinosaurs is a stegosaurus. In the summer of 2015, we were passing by these famous dinosaurs when Matthew stated the following, concerning the stegosaurus:

"Can I ride it? I want to smack it on the butt and call it Sally."

Matthew is hilarious.

Being entertaining is not his only prominent characteristic. Not unlike many of your experiences as a parent, Matthew teaches us things. One lesson that is applicable to real estate is that of *intensity* and *tenacity*. The kid is a master at not taking no for an answer.

Let's say that Matthew wants Chuck to throw the football with him. He'll start with the direct approach:

"Dad, will you throw the football with me?"

"No."

Matthew's response is not typical. He doesn't pout. He doesn't throw himself onto the floor with a tantrum. He doesn't put on the puppy dog face. He re-phrases the question.

"Do you think we can throw the football after I get ready for school?"

"No."

By now, most kids have tapped out. They have either given up or resorted to techniques that just get them in trouble. Not Matthew; he finds another approach.

"I'm ready for school. Let's just throw the football three times."

"No."

Matthew's in the big leagues now. There's not much competition world-wide. Only a few choice children dare to push any further, but Matthew's no amateur. He's a champion!

While Chuck is in the middle of trying to get some work done, Matthew throws the ball to Dad. Dad catches it, instinctively. Matthew says, "Let's see how many times we can catch it until one of us drops it." That's the sweet spot; he knows his father's competitiveness. Chuck can't resist, even if he wanted to.

What ensues is a throw and catch game that lasts much longer than three throws. Matthew just wouldn't accept "no."

Does it work every time for Matthew? Not at all! In fact, he experiences emphatic "no's" much more than the satisfying "yes's." However, he persists, and at a master level of skill.

Distinguishing "No" from "Not Yet"

Unlike most agents that give up after the first or second "no," this child has mastered the skill of knowing when "it's really not a *no*, it's a not yet," and he's an expert at either rephrasing questions or taking a specific action to get the result he wants. Furthermore, he does it tactfully, without getting himself in trouble. Matthew's masterful persistence is a lesson that most professional agents should take heed to.

This is the same kid who will go into school and sell paper cell phones for a profit. Here's the story:

Matthew is creative. Furthermore, he's a likeable kid, so other kids tend to listen to him. One day, Matthew brings home some money. He explains that he earned this money by selling cell phones.

"Cell phones?" I wondered, checking my purse.

No, not real ones: paper cell phones. Matthew drew them, cut them out and sold them. He even expanded his line to paper laptops. We couldn't believe it.

At one point, another kid saw the business that Matthew had and started up his own "paper electronics company." Matthew wanted no competition so he "made him an offer he couldn't refuse" and said, "Hey, listen! Either I will put you out of business or you can come sell for me." Now Matthew has an independent contractor working for him.

Gee, I wonder where Matthew could have gotten that skill.

When Chuck got wind of this, he had a talk with Matthew and said, "Do you think that's right taking kids' money for a paper phone?"

Matthew replied, "But Dad, they're willing to pay me for it."

Chuck said, "That's fine. But if any kid asks for his money back, you'd better give it to him."

Matthew agreed to the terms.

Matthew makes it clear that he is determined to make himself very successful at whatever he decides he's interested in. Chuck and I have this same trait. We sometimes wonder why some people have it and some people don't. As leaders, we always try to figure out how we can tap into this quality within the agents we work with.

We wish we could unzip people, stuff them with all that we know, zip them back up and send them on their way to success, but it just doesn't work that way. Regardless, we sure do try. That is one of the huge advantages agents that are working with our brokerage have. We are constantly stuffing our knowledge into our agents.

Decide to Thrive

Tenacity, creativity and the ability to look outside of the box can be learned skills. You can decide to be this type of agent.

Chuck and I had a land listing in a custom subdivision in Summerhill. We have only sold fifteen to twenty land sales in our entire career. All of these lots were in custom subdivisions, so it's not all that impressive since you don't really need to know a lot about land to sell a lot in a subdivided custom home community. However, out of these fifteen to twenty sales, eleven of them were our listings. Honestly, that's crazy, but it's true.

How did we sell them? We sat them open.

Yes, I'm talking about the lots—vacant land. We sat some of them open. It all started with the lot in Summerhill, which I'm not even sure we ever sold. Regardless, Chuck and I sat that lot open. People thought we were nuts.

When buyers are driving around looking at open houses, they are generally looking for *houses*. Can you imagine the reactions we got when people were following our "open house" signs and ended up at an empty lot with the two of us at a little table and two chairs?

When people would drive up to our table, we would talk to them, and guess what? We picked up business. We found buyers and sellers . . . go figure. The unique thing with holding a vacant lot open is that it's like pulling up to a drive-through window. Everyone talked to us. They didn't have to get out of their car, and it would have been super awkward for them to just drive away. They *all* talked to us. In fact, a great number of them talked for a long time. That's right: There's no such thing as typical in our book.

Creative, outside-the-box thinking allowed us to meet new people who were potential buyers and sellers. All we had to do is find out if they would be willing to let us help them, and a whole lot of them were. People recognize how hard you work and also the passion that you have.

One of our best stories about being creative, outside-the-box thinkers all started with a For Sale By Owner in Ahwatukee. We told you the story of Mark. The Mark story led us to an FSBO (which we listed and sold). After our initial appointment with that FSBO, Chuck and I were heading back to our car when an older couple approached us. The wife said something a bit peculiar. She said, "You look like a hot couple!" (That's not the peculiar part.) "We want you to sell our house."

We're thinking to ourselves, "Right on!" Well, I was thinking, "Right on!" but Chuck would never say "Right on." He's actually cool. He says cool things, and I am self-aware enough to know that "Right on!" is not a cool thing to say.

Anyway, we were both eager to hear them out. Turns out they had a home not far away that they wanted to sell. The catch was that they didn't want to have a "for sale" sign or a lockbox in their yard. They also didn't want the home in the multiple listing service. Furthermore, they didn't want anyone to walk through the home without an appointment and booties. (They had white, fancy carpet, the kind that families with kids *never* have.) Finally, they didn't want to sign any type of listing contract.

They wanted to sell their home with no sign, no lockbox, no exposure on the internet, no open houses, restrictions on showings and no contract commitment.

Chuck is the competitive one, so he said, "No problem! If anyone can do it, it will be us!" Chuck is notorious for taking on any challenge. I, on the other hand, was thinking, "How the heck are we going to pull this off?"

They brought us to look at their home. When I say it was pristine, that's a total understatement. The snow-white carpet was imported from Persia. They had furniture that had never been sat on; bathrooms that had never been used; an untouched stove, oven and microwave; and yes, they actually lived there. We had to wear booties, and their grandchildren weren't even allowed inside the house. They were willing to pay us a commission if we could sell the home, and they agreed to buy their next house with us, which, by the way, was going to be a 1.5 million dollar home.

We sold the home. As it turned out, the price they wanted was super reasonable, and we found an investor willing to buy it. The couple also did buy a home for $1.4 million, but that wasn't the craziest part. These people had family . . . a lot of family! For the next two years, we helped their family members buy and sell. They came out of the woodwork. They *always* bought brand new, absolutely refusing to live in a used home. When they sold, almost all of them had pristine homes with some furniture that was never sat on.

It was unbelievable how much business we got from this family, and it's all because we took that first risk. You never know the waterfall of business that will come from one encounter. Have an open mind. Work excellently! Be tenacious!

Look, There's a Butterfly! A Lesson in Focus

There's an adorable little creature called the bushy-tailed woodrat that has large, round ears; super long whiskers; a tiny nose and a bushy tail like a squirrel. One of the common names for them is a pack rat because while many animals make nests containing all kinds of natural materials, the woodrat not only gathers natural materials into its nest but also shiny objects . . . basically, anything it can find. I have read stories of all kinds of crazy shiny objects that have been found in their nests: anything from tinfoil and bottle caps to watches and diamonds.

One behavior of the woodrat that I found very interesting gives this little rodent another common name: trade rat. Here's what they do: sometimes, the woodrat will find an object it likes and pick it up. The intent (because I speak woodrat) is to bring that prized object into the nest. However, on the way to the nest, the woodrat might spy an object it seems to like even better. Instead of noting the location of this second desirable object and completing the task of bringing the first object to the nest, Mr. Trade Rat will drop the first treasure found and pick up the second, leaving the first behind. This behavior can happen several times on the way back to the nest.

The woodrat may have had a perfectly wonderful addition for the nest but gets distracted by the next shiny object it sees. Consequently, the first item is dropped completely and forgotten. The second object may last no longer.

If we speak metaphorically about a successful agent's business, their "nest" should be made with the materials that make a good nest: prospecting, follow up, appointments and contracts. Successful agents hone in on certain key things in each of these categories and stay consistent and persistent in these activities and practices. Their nest becomes strong and produces.

However, some real estate agents can be pack rats. Instead of building their business with the materials it takes to build a strong business, they clutter their nests with all kinds of shiny objects.

We get it. The shiny objects are so pretty. Prospecting and follow up, for example, are not so pretty. Apps and promises of internet leads seem so sparkly, so enchanting.

Many REALTORS® have actually heard the truth: You need to get out there and prospect! Door knock, open house, call expired listings and FSBOs! Get face-to-face and on-the-phone contacts with new people so you can find those buyers and sellers willing to work with you! But then, Mr. Trade Rat REALTOR®, while carrying that truth back to his nest, gets distracted by an appealing, colorful, easier shiny object and drops the first, proven business-building method for the second bright shiny object.

When our 17-year-old son, David, was four years old, he played baseball. Sometimes David would be very interested in the game . . . *sometimes*. However, then there would be a butterfly or a bee or a dragonfly or something really interesting in the grass. Suddenly the game just wasn't at all important. To watch this from the sidelines was super entertaining. We laughed, and it's a great story to tell.

Take it from us: When Chuck and I are watching from the sidelines at some agents jumping through the field of the real estate business trying to catch the butterflies, only to be distracted by the shiny object, it's not so cute.

Don't think of it as boring to prospect, follow up and repeat, over and over and over again. Those are the activities that are the building blocks to a lucrative real estate career. Get focused! Be tenacious!

Don't be a bushy-tailed woodrat.

Chuck says:

> I am constantly telling our agents that there is no easy way to success. We are distracted by these shiny objects believing that this may be it or that may be the answer! Then I don't have to work hard! *No!* The success shortcut doesn't exist. Nothing replaces hard work and passion for doing it. Embrace the process!

———

1. *Can you think of ways you need to improve yourself in terms of intention, intensity and focus?*

2. *Can you identify things in your life that get in the way of these things?*

3. *Do you know anyone who does a great job in these areas?*

CHAPTER ELEVEN

EMBRACE THE PROCESS

I t's always great to achieve and complete a goal. However, the process of getting there is much longer than the moment of achievement. If you cannot embrace the process by enjoying and appreciating not only the reward or accomplishment but also the journey getting there, you will spend most of your life striving for short moments of happiness. If you can really wrap your mind around the importance of embracing the process, you will begin to live your life with more passion and joy.

There are many things that can get in the way of you enjoying the journey. One of the obvious obstacles is that you aren't in a career that suits you. Remember Mark Manson's article? Do you *really* want to do what you're doing? For some, real estate is not where you should be. Get out and do something you're passionate about. Let's assume you are in the correct career.

What obstacles get in the way of embracing the process? You've already read about some of them. Some are mindset issues or unrealistic expectations.

Another thing to consider is that for many people who are only focused on the destination, enjoying the journey is out of the question. The process seems mundane, repetitive, unappealing, grueling and a laundry list of other depressing descriptors. When you cannot embrace the process, which is the journey, other feelings creep in and take control of your life. They are not productive feelings. They are destructive.

It reminds me of a poem by Shel Silverstein called "Lazy Jane" that talks about a girl who's so lazy that when she's thirsty she waits for it to rain instead of getting herself a drink of water.

As a child, I really loved Shel's poems in his *Where the Sidewalk Ends* book. I used to taunt my sister with the poem, "For Sale," that starts off talking about a crying and spying young sister for sale. You get the point. Let's get back to Jane. She's lazy.

Thirsty Jane is so lazy she just lies down waiting for the rain! She would probably be okay in Seattle, but in Phoenix she'd be a goner! I know you're going to find this hard to believe, but there are a lot of lazy Janes in real estate. But instead of waiting for it to rain, lazy agents look at Facebook, read their email and complain about not making any money!

Combating laziness is what all successful people do. Laziness not only hinders the success of agents but also doesn't serve our clients well. Lazy agents are the ones who remove the key from the lockbox before closing, without seller permission, because they don't want to drive "all the way back to the house" again.

Our average sales price currently is over $250,000. The average commission earned is about 3%, making the gross commission on the average house over $7,500! Really, and you can't drive back to the house one more time to do things the right way? Laziness is hard to swallow.

That same lazy agent might not even show up to the inspection if the buyers aren't going. They won't bother to read the preliminary title report or review the Seller Property Disclosures . . . *so* much reading! They'll fill in that one missing initial that their client missed, and what's a little white-out between friends? Laziness is hard to swallow.

When laziness settles in, it becomes like a ball and chain on an agent's business. It's really hard to do the activities you need to do to make money. We don't mean difficult, per se, but hard in other ways. Picking up the phone and calling expired listings takes some rhinoceros skin. Think about it! Expired listings didn't sell. Are those sellers more likely to be happy their house didn't sell or upset at some level? Furthermore, they are probably upset at their agent, which quickly becomes frustration with all agents. You have to pump yourself up to make those calls while sounding positive and energetic. It helps to come armed with polished scripts and objection-busting skills, but those take work. Being lazy and being effective don't go together.

Expose Your Inner Laziness

Are you lazy? Here are some steps you should take to find out. First, do you have a schedule written down (or in a program)? I'm not talking about a schedule in your head but actually written down. If you don't have a *recorded* schedule, you're probably lazy. "Oh, Angela! That's not an indication of laziness!" Yes, it is.

Definition of lazy: Not liking to work hard or be active; disinclined to activity or exertion.

If you don't have a recorded schedule, ask yourself why not? The simple answer is that it's work to write down a schedule. It's not even hard work, which really shows how lazy we are. Writing a schedule is also a commitment. Lazy people don't commit.

Let's say you do have a schedule. The next step is to look at what's in it. Is it a weenie schedule or a robust one that sets you up for success? If you are a full-time real estate agent, 50-60% of your time, or twenty to twenty-five hours per week, should be in dollar-producing activities such as:

- Prospecting (face to face or on the phone)

- Follow up (face to face or on the phone)

- Setting/attending appointments (with buyers and/or sellers)

- Listing homes

- Writing purchase contracts

- Closing homes

Nothing else counts. These are the activities crucial to making money in real estate. If your schedule doesn't include these activities, you're probably lazy. Lazy people won't even write down and plan for these activities.

Let's say you actually do have a robust schedule for yourself. The next step to take is to evaluate your adherence to this schedule. At the end of each day, you should review your accomplishments. If you had three hours of prospecting blocked out on your schedule, did you actually spend three hours doing this? For example, if you had three hours of door knocking planned from 1:00-4:00 p.m., did you knock on your first door at 1:00 and your last at 4:00? In between 1:00-4:00, were you moving efficiently from house to house, conversation to conversation, without interruption?

Or did you start preparing for your door knocking at 1:00 by printing out some materials and then did you drive around looking for where you want to start? Was it 1:30 (or later) before you finally got to the first door? Then, maybe you took several phone calls in between houses. Around 2:45, you might have realized you forgot to do a couple of things that you decided were really important, so you left the neighborhood, saying to yourself that you would make up the last hour another day.

Another example could be if you committed to calling some people in your center of influence for two hours from 3:00-5:00 p.m. Did you determine who you would call ahead of time and have all of their information ready by 3:00? Did you decide on the intent of your phone calls? Were your conversations upbeat and helpful? Did you ask for business? Were you efficient in your conversations with at least ten to fifteen contacts?

Or was it more like at 3:00, you opened your contacts in your phone, scrolling down to a name you could call? That person didn't answer, so you thought of another person but their contact information wasn't in your phone. You looked in your email to find the phone number. When you were about to search for the contact's name, you noticed an email marked "URGENT." You quickly read over the email and then made a phone call to answer the question. At 3:25, you remembered who you were trying to look up and found their number. Great news! The person answers the phone, and you chat for thirty minutes about the vacation they just took. You hang up without asking for business or adding any value to them as a real estate agent.

You may be thinking, "But Angela, I built great rapport with them." Good for you. They'll be sure to think of you when they want to chat again. However, they'll call a REALTOR® when they want to sell their home.

At 4:00, you scroll through your contacts again. Just then, the washing machine chimes that it's done, so you jump up quickly to throw the load into the dryer so it doesn't start to stink. On the way back to your desk, you grab a snack and a drink. You can't really eat while you're talking on the phone, so it's 4:30 before you're ready to get back down to your "hard work."

Because committing to a schedule *is* hard work. Hard work is the opposite of lazy. If you find yourself half-heartedly doing the dollar-producing activities on your schedule, you're probably lazy.

Now that you have taken some steps to determine your level of laziness, what can you do to combat it? Keep in mind that everyone has some level of laziness, so don't beat yourself up too much (or do, if you're too lazy to do anything about it!).

Just Get Started (with a Prosperous Morning Routine)

The hardest part of a tough or mundane task is simply getting started. Having a "just get started" mindset is powerful and starts first thing in the morning. I'm sure you've heard time and time again how incredibly important it is to have a strong morning routine. Starting your day off in a spectacular way will set the tone for the rest of the day. Here are some possible elements to an amazing morning routine:

- Jump out of bed! You can take this literally, which gets your blood flowing for sure, or at least break the habit of hitting that snooze button. Hitting the snooze button starts your day off with procrastination. Just get up!

- Exercise—Whether it's ten minutes of stretching or forty-five minutes of hard exercise, making this part of your morning routine can give you the mental and physical boost you need to attack the day.

- Spend some time focusing on positive things. Hopefully, you have goals. They should be written down. Many of the successful agents we know also have vision boards where they place goals and visual representations of what they are trying to achieve. Part of your morning can be spent looking at and reviewing these. Prayer and/or meditation can be great. Listening to positive, motivational speakers or reading something inspirational can set your mind on the right track, too.

- Make your morning media-free. Not only do you need to fill your mind with positive things, but you must also protect your mind from things that bring you down. The news and most talk radio is depressing. Stay away from it!

- Spend some time thinking about the things for which you are grateful. Gratitude is such a powerful mindset and charges your brain to have the right outlook on the day.

Having a "just get started" mindset can definitely start in the morning but can also pervade the rest of your day. Feeling lazy-minded about prospecting? Just get started! If it's door knocking, simply getting dressed and knocking on that first door is likely to roll into more and more doors. Our minds are funny. It's almost like we make things into much bigger deals than they really are. Most of the time, after you finish a task you were dreading, you look back and honestly say, "That really wasn't that bad."

Eliminate Distractions

I can only imagine the enormous amount of time we waste due to distractions. Left unchecked, everyone will fall victim to being sidetracked. It's all of our natural default. Laziness is attracted to distraction. Therefore, if you are combating laziness, you have to make a conscious effort to eliminate distractions.

Distractions come in all shapes and sizes. There are obvious distractions, such as people interrupting your work time with gossip. However, there are less obvious distractions that disguise themselves as important. For example, let's say you are in the middle of a difficult transaction, and you're waiting to find out some important news from the lender about an appraisal. It's your prospecting time, and you are supposed to be making calls to your center of influence. You see that the lender is calling you.

That call is a distraction. If you answer that call, you have mislabeled it as important. The reason it's mislabeled is because of the answer to this question:

If I find out the answer right now or two hours from now, will it make any difference at all?

Chances are, the answer is *no*! Therefore, if you are supposed to be laser-focused on prospecting, and you allow that phone call to throw you off track, you've been distracted.

Eliminating distractions takes practice. It's taking the time to be aware of the choices you're making. It takes discipline to do things like turn your computer screen and phone off while working on a project. However, the payoff is enormous. Blocks of time without distractions will result in more efficiency and a higher level of results. A higher level of results leads to heightened satisfaction. When you are satisfied, you are more likely to repeat the actions that produced those results.

Write a Schedule and Journal

Simply writing down what needs to get done in time blocks is a huge benefit for your business. There is a whole lot of information about how to schedule. Just Google it. Getting into how to schedule is not the point of this chapter. The point is you need a schedule—no way around it! Without a schedule, you cannot possibly be successful in real estate.

Following the schedule is a whole other challenge. It's easy to let day after day go by feeling busy but not really accomplishing the most important tasks on your schedule. Journaling at the end of the day is an excellent way to measure yourself in terms of true productivity. It doesn't have to take more than a few minutes. At the end of the day, write down only the truly important things you accomplished. Don't write down the excuses or explanations.

The results in your journal will tell you all you need to know about how well you have adhered to your schedule (assuming your schedule is robust and appropriate).

Find Accountability Partners

Almost everyone needs accountability to be successful. I want to say *everyone* needs this but, since I haven't met everyone, I'll say almost everyone. Chuck and I are accountability partners. We push each other to move forward, take action and follow through. I know that we wouldn't be where we are today without each other. Being accountable wards off laziness.

As a REALTOR®, it is easy to not do what it takes to be successful. You probably won't be fired if you don't. It's just not like that. You'll be broke, but probably not fired. The very best thing you can do for yourself and the success of your business is to have more than one accountability partner. This person might prospect with you. Several of our more successful agents will have daily morning check-ins to tell each other what they will accomplish that day, and then they'll circle back around at the end of the day to report results.

Another thing to do to hold yourself accountable is to make your schedule public. If you have an office at your brokerage, post it on your door. Announce it to your family. Give a copy to your broker or office manager. Making your schedule public usually forces you to actually make a schedule that isn't awful. You're also more likely to follow that schedule, especially if the people to whom you make your schedule public are likely to ask you about your day.

Again, combating laziness is what all successful people do. Remember, each person is inclined toward laziness. You are not unique in this problem. Fight it!

Chuck says:

> How do you know you're lazy? Are you that agent who likes to talk and gossip all day? Are you one of those agents who is constantly scrolling through Facebook, Instagram and Snapchat? Are you one of those agents who joined a company just because it seems fun? The good news is that you can combat lazy. Taking small bites in terms of good activities can start to create a good habit. When Angela and I first started prospecting, we didn't make some big master plan. We just woke up each day and decided to do it. It wasn't long before prospecting was such a habit that we felt guilty if we *weren't* prospecting. It became second nature to us, and with a little commitment, success activities can become second nature to you too.

There's Nothing New Under The Sun (But You Can Still Soar Miles Above Other Agents)

Aside from being lazy, failing to embrace the process can cause you to constantly search for that magic pill, that easier way. If you pay attention to many agents who are unsuccessful, you will see them often acting like that bushy-tailed woodrat we talked about in chapter ten. The lack of focus can be a symptom of the failure to embrace the process.

> **"What has been is what will be, and what has been done is what will be done, and there is nothing new under the sun."**
>
> ECCLESIASTES 1:9
> [ENGLISH STANDARD VERSION]

I was once preparing for a presentation to a group of agents focused on becoming excellent listing agents. I had presented to this group six other times and this was the last in the series, so I was looking for something *amazing*! I wanted something that would rock their real estate world, catapult them to the next level and leave them gasping for air. First, I spent some time trying to think about how to end the series. I had nothing, so what did I do? That's right; I Googled.

Forty-five minutes later, I thought to myself, "There's nothing new to talk about . . . nothing at all."

Real estate is just not that complicated. You have to find people who are looking to buy or sell. They have to want to work with you. You help them buy or sell and then, when the home closes, you make money.

The process can be described that simply. Don't get me wrong! Being an amazing, professional REALTOR® takes an expertise in so many different areas that not many rise to this level. There is a huge difference between an experienced, professional agent and all the others. When Chuck or I are working a deal against a less-experienced agent or an agent with lesser skills, I can tell you for a fact that the other agent's client suffers. Most clients have absolutely no idea that their agent has that profound of an effect on their transaction.

Furthermore, if one of our agents contacts us about a problem in their transaction and our agent fully takes our counsel, the other agent's client suffers. We are simply experienced enough to be that skilled.

However, fundamentally, there's not that much to talk about when it comes to being a successful real estate agent. Remember:

"What has been is what will be, and what has been done is what will be done, and there is nothing new under the sun" (Ecclesiastes 1:9 [English Standard Version]).

God's got it right! There is nothing new, and you're no different. Some people may find that statement depressing, thinking, "What? I'm not special? I'm not the exception? I don't have the capacity to do something fundamentally different in real estate? I'm not going to be the '*the one*' who finds the magic pill? I'm not 'the one' who finds a better way, an easier way?"

NO!

You're not the exception. You're not.

I'm not saying that you cannot set yourself apart from other agents. You absolutely can! Like I said before, Chuck and I will run circles around most agents, and you can too. But, "running circles around" other agents has nothing to do with something new under the sun.

The Exact Steps to Become a Top-Notch Agent

If you would like to be one of those agents who rise above, you need to take several steps on a regular basis. Here are a few of them:

Schedule with quality, and follow it! As addressed in a previous chapter, proper scheduling and follow-through is imperative for the successful real estate agent.

Learn the contract paperwork. No matter where you practice real estate, there is paperwork to learn. In Arizona, agents are permitted to actually write contracts, therefore acting like attorneys in this limited scope. No matter how much paperwork you are directly facilitating, you should know it. That takes training and effort.

Practice and hone your skills. There are so many different skills you can practice to be exceptional. Here are a couple of crucial areas to focus on:

- Scripts—Scripts are simply templates to help you deliver information. Well-formed scripts include effective words, questions that seek helpful information, and great closing questions. There are many effectively written scripts that you can find pertaining to real estate. Our recommendation would be to start with those. Scripts allow you to deliver information in a predictable and productive way.

  There are effective scripts for everything you do in real estate, including: prospecting, negotiating, making presentations, busting objections, and much more. Whether or not you purposefully seek great scripts to learn and master, you will use scripts. The problem is, if you don't seek, learn and master appropriate scripts, yours will probably not be as effective as they could be.

- Non verbal communication—Just as important as *what* you say is *how* you say it. Learning skills in intonation, for example, can cause you to sound better. Your body language can empower you to seem more confident or speak volumes about your lack thereof. How you mirror people can allow you to seem more appealing. All of these things can be learned and mastered through practice.

Serve. We are in a business of customer service. If you give your clients an experience with great communication and amazing service, you will set yourself apart. Most people just won't go through the trouble of truly serving their clients.

Buying or selling a home, or doing both at the same time as some people do, ranks as one of the top most stressful events a person can experience in their lifetime. To put it into perspective, here are some other things that are on that same list:

- Getting married
- Getting divorced
- Death in the family
- Losing a job or some other financial trauma
- Major sickness
- Having a baby
- Empty nest syndrome.

When you look at these other incredibly stressful life events, guess what often occurs at the same time? You guessed it: home purchase or sale. If you consider that people are experiencing one or more of their most stressful events all at once, it begins to be clear how important the concept of great service becomes. Over the years, I have talked so many clients off the edge by listening intently to the stress that they feel so that they would remain comfortable and confident through the process.

When you're dealing with really stressed-out clients, do you think you see their best side or something less than that? Of course they are not at their best! There are so many agents that get aggravated at their clients for being *human*. You have to have a humble, caring servant's heart to help these people through.

A lot of agents believe that technology will take over real estate in the future—a future where agents are obsolete. We believe agents with these beliefs are the same agents who don't excel or even give good customer service. Real estate is a face-to-face business. If you have great customer service and know your stuff, you will always have clients. We, as a company, get this. That is why we have systems in place to give our agents' clients top-notch service even after the transaction. Our clients become *Revelation Platinum Club Members,* and we make sure that we keep in touch and offer value.

The elements of setting yourself apart don't ever come to an end. What I mean is that many unbelievable REALTORS® practice their scripts every day. They don't feel like they've arrived and can stop practicing. They're never done with training and improving themselves. They are professionals, and professionals continually work on their craft. Professionals realize that although they can always improve and refine, they will have to continue to repeat and repeat the same basic activities to stay on top of their game.

Prospecting will always be the process of meeting new people so that you can find buyers and/or sellers willing to work with you. Follow-up will always be where you make most of your appointments. You are going to have to go on appointments so that you can write contracts. Close them, and you'll make money.

1. *Can you sense the importance of embracing the process?*

2. *In which ways will you need to push yourself in order to embrace the process?*

3. *Will you decide today that you will enjoy both the journey and the destination?*

CHAPTER TWELVE

GETTING TO THE NEXT LEVEL

Real estate is such a fantastic career. There are so many ways to grow and improve—so many different directions you can take things over the span of your career. One of the most rewarding parts of Chuck's and my position is the opportunity to help agents get to the next level.

Getting to the next level can mean many different things for a real estate agent, including:

- Increasing your production

- Starting a team

- Improving your closing statistics

- Moving from being an agent into being a member of the brokerage's staff

- Moving from being a member of the staff to being an agent

- Becoming a mentor of newer or struggling agents

- Instructing new or struggling agents

Since Chuck and I started in this field, we've been agents, team leaders, mentors, coaches, instructors, managers, owners of a brokerage, developers of a real estate school—and that's just a partial list. This is exciting stuff!

Regardless of what your "next level" looks like, there are some qualities you should develop within yourself to help you succeed. Brendon Burchard, an author, coach and motivational speaker, has spent years studying high-performance in people. He has many great insights into what makes a person succeed in a sustained, consistent and high-level way. One of the qualities he describes is the importance of confidence. In his study, he looked at many indicators that successful people possess, and the concept of confidence was of paramount importance and correlated strongly to positively affecting these indicators. This is the statement that Brendon asked high performers to rate themselves on:

I have confidence in my ability to achieve my goals despite obstacles.

The higher they indicated that this statement was true for them, the more the indicators were positively affected. I'm not surprised about this. Confidence is a choice. Brendon speaks of a confidence competence cycle. The way you build your confidence is by challenging yourself. When you do, and come out the other side, you have learned things, and your confidence can grow. When you're more competent, you seek out more challenges, and the cycle begins. Chuck and I have confidence. I know that a challenge can be thrown our way and no matter whether or not we have any experience or skill set with regards to the challenge, we can figure it out together. We *love* the challenge!

Toes on the Edge of a Cliff

In 2004, just a few short years into our real estate business, we stumbled upon an opportunity. This is what happened.

Chuck was showing clients new builds in south Chandler. South Chandler was about twenty minutes away from where we were currently living. He called me excitedly about a home he saw.

The background is that we had been looking for a new house. In fact, we were really close to accepting a counter for a house both Chuck and I really loved in Ahwatukee. However, we prayed about it overnight and both woke up knowing that it wasn't the house we were supposed to move into.

So, Chuck dropped off the south Chandler clients and picked me up right away. The new build was amazing, and after prayerful consideration, we moved forward on that house. We moved in January of 2005. That was the year we sold almost forty million in real estate. At that time in our career, 90% of our business was in Ahwatukee. Within three months of moving to Chandler, 90% of our business was happening in Chandler. It was nothing short of miraculous, and we felt sure we had made the right move.

We were commuting to the Ahwatukee office, which was only about twenty-five minutes away, but one day, Chuck called the owner of the brokerage we currently worked for and said, "When are you going to open an office in south Chandler? We don't want to commute."

At the time, we were that company's number one agents out of 3500 agents. We were already in the top 1% of agents in the nation. I guess, because of that, the owner said, "Why don't you open an office in south Chandler?"

Remember, we were explaining in an earlier chapter the importance of working thoughtfully through your business. Opening a new brokerage is a big deal, and neither of us had any business experience. Since I loved school and Chuck hated school, I was the clear choice to go back to school and learn about business. We also hired a strategic planner to help us to create a business plan and a coach to support us as we lay the foundation of the infrastructure of our new business endeavor. We consulted our accountant before developing our business budget . . . blah blah blah.

Stop right there! Actually, we weren't smart enough to be that thoughtful. Not at all. Let's rewind and try that again. The truth, this time.

The owner said, "Why don't you open an office in south Chandler?"

We said, "Okay."

Honestly, that's how it went. Chuck and I—a couple of inexperienced business people—set out to open a brokerage.

We knew less about opening a business than we did about real estate when we first started. I didn't even have my broker's license. I asked Charlie, the very talented woman who helped us run our team, "Hey Charlie, want to get your broker's license with me and open up a brokerage?"

To our team members, we said, "Want to come and work at our new brokerage?"

I wish we could tell you that our process was more sophisticated. It was not. Charlie and I got our broker's licenses, and in November of 2005, our brokerage was born.

Starting our real estate brokerage was extremely challenging. We had absolutely no idea what we were doing in starting a business. We were really great at selling real estate and motivating agents; therefore, our training was good. We recruited really well, and our environment was upbeat and positive. We grew quickly. We've been open twelve years now, and the process has had our toes off the edge of a cliff over and over again. We haven't overcome and succeeded in the face of every challenge, and we've made a ton of mistakes. However, our confidence and the willingness to continually step back into a challenge has greatly contributed to our success. If you want to get to another level, you too must face challenges that are hard and scary. There is no getting around it.

Just Move the Chair

Chuck and I were in a restaurant not too long ago. We wanted to sit outside as it was a beautiful day. (By the way, almost every day is beautiful in Arizona, but I digress.) The hostess led us out to the patio to a table for two. It was seemingly the only space available. The problem was that the misters were dripping water onto the little table, and it was a tight squeeze being so close to the railing and other tables.

Chuck looked up toward a great outdoor bar. The bar was a large rectangle with two sides inside the restaurant and two sides out. It was much more spacious and clearly a more comfortable choice. Chuck and I walked over to see if there was space for us there.

One side was completely full. When we turned the corner, there was only one vacant chair on the other side.

I truly believe that most people would have just moved back to the less desirable spot. Not Chuck. He simply squeezed past all the people again, grabbed one of the chairs from the first spot, carried it over his head and put it at the bar. He left one opportunity and created a new, better one, and for the next two hours, we enjoyed the better one.

Think about it. All it took was an open-enough mind and a little risk taking. All he did was take a chair and move it to another spot and our whole experience was enhanced. What was the actual risk? The hostess or waitress telling us that we can't move the chair? This is not much of a risk, but the truth is, most people are afraid to even take the smallest risk.

In the real estate industry, there are so many parallels to draw to "just moving the chair." First of all, taking a moment to analyze your situation and asking yourself how you can "just move the chair" to better your situation is an amazing opportunity. For example, let's say that you aren't satisfied with your average sales price and would like to work with clients in a higher price range. How can you "just move the chair" in this situation? It could be as easy as sitting open houses at a higher price point.

How can open houses at a higher price point help? Let's say that your average sales price is $250,000. If you start sitting open houses that are at least $400,000, you will have people who walk in and say to you, "Oh, we can't afford this price range. We're only approved for $325,000." Your response should be, "Well, that's no problem! There are a lot of amazing deals out there in your price range." Tada! You have just upped your average price range. Imagine if you sat homes in the $500,000 range? In this situation, you are literally "moving your chair" from a lower-price-point open house to a higher one.

Another example would be if you are dissatisfied with the number of referrals or repeat business you are receiving. In this example of "just moving your chair," you should analyze what you're doing right now to build relationship with your center of influence. Are you really doing all you can to stay in the forefront of these people's minds? Are you delivering the highest level of service and value to them? Are you giving them a reason to think of you when they are looking to buy or sell or when they hear about someone looking to buy or sell?

This version of "moving your chair" may involve revamping your systems and procedures concerning your center of influence. Do you celebrate important events in their lives in a meaningful way? Do you call them on their birthdays? Do you send them items of value? What are you doing to create relationship and reinforce your success in the business? Staying in the forefront of their minds demands thoughtful process and procedure, along with a heart looking to serve your clients. Making adjustments in this area can completely transform your business and get you to a new level.

The concept of moving your chair should be a part of the regular analysis of your business. Taking the time to consider each part of your business, looking for opportunities to improve, to expand or rework, can cause growth. Sometimes it's the small adjustments that can make a huge difference, but you have to take the time to figure out what they should be.

Chuck says:

> Agents say they want different results, but wishful thinking gets you nowhere. Take some actions! There are so many things you can do that will give you different results. Remember, we were broke and ready to get out of the business. A series of different actions, consistently and persistently executed, gave us superior success.

You Need Great People Speaking into Your Life

In conclusion, we want to reiterate the importance of having quality people around you. Getting to the next level can be accomplished to some degree alone, but I've never met a single person who would consider themselves really successful who proclaimed to do it all alone. Without my husband, there is no way I'd be where I am in my life, and I know that he feels the same way.

In 2016, I asked Chuck to take me to Dave Ramsey's EntreLeadership Master Series. It was literally a game-changer for us and our business. We used that opportunity to its fullest potential and "surrounded" ourselves with Dave Ramsey and his EntreLeadership concepts. The reason I told you this is because you have to open up your mind to how you can surround yourself with amazing people, too. Dave Ramsey is not a personal friend of ours, although it was super cool to have dinner at his house. However, we allow his organization to speak into our life through that Master Series event, books, videos and the Entre-Leadership podcasts.

Once you have opened your mind to how to grab this experience, you'll quickly see how accessible this blessing is, and it will most definitely help you get to the next level. You should be reading great books, listening to amazing podcasts, attending seminars—feed your mind. Our prayer is that this book has spoken blessings into your life. We hope it has inspired your passion for learning more about the exciting and fulfilling path to success in the real estate industry. Real estate is an amazing career, and you can master it!

—

1. *If you are already in real estate, what is your next level?*

2. *Can you identify times in your life where you took risks and came out the other side of it more confident and competent?*

3. *Who in your life challenges you to be the best version of yourself?*

FINAL WORD FROM THE AUTHORS

Thank you for reading! We hope you've found *Mastering Your Real Estate Career* helpful. We'd love to hear any questions, comments, and/or success stories you may have; please feel free to send them to us at MasteringYourRealEstateCareer@gmail.com.

Lastly, we cannot stress enough the importance of aligning yourself with a brokerage that will provide the tools, training, and support you need to succeed. As a reminder, here are the brokerage interview questions you will need to ask before making your decision:

1. What type of training can I expect to receive?

2. Do you have a mentorship program? If yes, what does it entail? Who are your mentors and what success have they experienced in real estate?

3. Who are the instructors? What makes them qualified to teach those courses? What success have they experienced in real estate?

4. Is there a training class I could sit in on before making a decision about your brokerage?

5. Who are the brokers? What success have they experienced in real estate? How accessible are the brokers? How do I reach them?

6. How does your brokerage keep agents informed about the industry and the market?

7. May I have a copy of your agent roster so that I can ask some of them questions about what it's like to work here?

8. What tools and systems do you offer?

May God bless your real estate career!

*To book Chuck and Angela Fazio
for a speaking event, send an email to
MasteringYourRealEstateCareer@gmail.com.*

BIBLIOGRAPHY

Ellen Horowitz , "Bushy-tailed Woodrat," *Montana Outdoors* (blog), accessed August 28, 2017, *http://fwp.mt.gov/mtoutdoors/ HTML/articles/portraits/woodrat.htm.*

Edward William Bok, *The Americanization of Edward Bok* (Pennsylvania, 1920).

Mark Manson, "The Most Important Question of Your Life," *Mark Manson* (blog), November 6, 2013, *http://markmanson.net/ question.*

Melissa Breyer, "What's Really Inside? The Anatomy of a Hot Dog," *TreeHugger* (blog), June 30, 2016, *http://www.treehugger. com/green-food/anatomy-hot-dog-whats-inside.html.*

Sara Roncero-Menendez, "In Defense Of Hot Dogs, America's Most Underrated Meat," *HuffPost* (blog), last modified August 7, 2014, *http://www.huffingtonpost.com/2014/07/02/ defense-of-hot-dogs_n_5534938.html.*

Shel Silverstein, "For Sale," *Where the Sidewalk Ends*, [New York: HarperCollins, 1974].

Shel Silverstein, "Lazy Jane," *Where the Sidewalk Ends*, [New York: HarperCollins, 1974].

"Getting Rockets into Space," *Science Learning Hub* (blog), last modified August 27, 2017, *http://sciencelearn.org.nz/Contexts/ Rockets/Looking-Closer/Getting-rockets-into-space.*

Made in the USA
San Bernardino, CA
26 February 2020

64985765R00091